SECOND EDITION

TOUCHSTONE

WORKBOOK 1

MICHAEL MCCARTHY
JEANNE MCCARTEN
HELEN SANDIFORD

CAMBRIDGE
UNIVERSITY PRESS

Shaftesbury Road, Cambridge CB2 8EA, United Kingdom

One Liberty Plaza, 20th Floor, New York, NY 10006, USA

477 Williamstown Road, Port Melbourne, VIC 3207, Australia

314–321, 3rd Floor, Plot 3, Splendor Forum, Jasola District Centre, New Delhi – 110025, India

103 Penang Road, #05-06/07, Visioncrest Commercial, Singapore 238467

Torre de los Parques, Colonia Tlacoquemécatl del Valle, Mexico City CP 03200, Mexico

Cambridge University Press & Assessment is a department of the University of Cambridge.

We share the University's mission to contribute to society through the pursuit of education, learning and research at the highest international levels of excellence.

www.cambridge.org
Information on this title: www.cambridge.org/9781107639331

© Cambridge University Press & Assessment 2005, 2014

This publication is in copyright. Subject to statutory exception and to the provisions of relevant collective licensing agreements, no reproduction of any part may take place without the written permission of Cambridge University Press & Assessment.

First published 2005
Second Edition 2014

20

Printed in Great Britain by Ashford Colour Press Ltd.

A catalog record for this publication is available from the British Library.

ISBN 978-1-107-67987-0 Student's Book
ISBN 978-1-107-62792-5 Student's Book A
ISBN 978-1-107-65345-0 Student's Book B
ISBN 978-1-107-63933-1 Workbook
ISBN 978-1-107-67071-6 Workbook A
ISBN 978-1-107-69125-4 Workbook B
ISBN 978-1-107-68330-3 Full Contact
ISBN 978-1-107-66769-3 Full Contact A
ISBN 978-1-107-61366-9 Full Contact B
ISBN 978-1-107-64223-2 Teacher's Edition with Assessment Audio CD/CD-ROM
ISBN 978-1-107-61414-7 Class Audio CDs (4)

Additional resources for this publication at www.cambridge.org/touchstone2

Cambridge University Press & Assessment has no responsibility for the persistence or accuracy of URLs for external or third-party internet websites referred to in this publication, and does not guarantee that any content on such websites is, or will remain, accurate or appropriate. Information regarding prices, travel timetables, and other factual information given in this work is correct at the time of first printing but Cambridge University Press & Assessment does not guarantee the accuracy of such information thereafter.

Contents

1 Meetings and greetings

Vocabulary | **A** Complete the conversations. Choose and write the best response.

1. A Hello.
   B _Hi._
   ⓐ Hi.
   b. Good-bye.

2. A Hi. I'm Ted.
   B _____
   a. Hi, I'm Lucille. Nice to meet you.
   b. See you next week.

3. A How are you?
   B _____
   a. I'm Kyle.
   b. I'm fine, thanks.

4. A Good-bye.
   B _____
   a. See you later.
   b. Thanks.

5. A Good night.
   B _____
   a. Hello.
   b. Bye. See you tomorrow.

6. A Hi. How are you?
   B _____
   a. Good, thanks. How are you?
   b. Have a nice day.

Vocabulary **B** Complete the conversations with the expressions in the box.

Good night.	✓Hello.	How are you?	Nice to meet you.
Have a good evening.	Hi.	I'm fine	See you

1. Jack ___*Hello.*___ I'm Jack.

   Anna _____ I'm Anna.

   Jack _____

2. Sonia Hi, Julie. How are you?

   Julie Good. _____

   Sonia _____ , thanks.

3. Mike _____

   Koji Thanks. You too.

4. Joan _____

   Mary Bye. _____ tomorrow.

C Complete the instant message.

Instant Message   ▭ ◰ ✕

Sandra Good morning, Jenny.

Jenny ___*Good morning*___ , Sandra.

Sandra _____ are you?

Jenny _____ , thanks. _____

Sandra Good.

Jenny See you later.

Sandra OK. _____ a nice day.

Jenny Thanks. _____ too.

Sandra Bye.

3

1 My name's Eva.

Vocabulary | Complete the conversation.

A   Good morning.

B   Good morning.

A   How are you?

B   I'm fine.

A   What's your __name__?

B   Eva Salazar.

A   How do you spell your _____ name?

B   It's S-A-L-A-Z-A-R.

A   And what's your _____ name?

B   Eva.

A   OK. How do you _____ *Eva*?

B   E-V-A.

A   And are you Ms., Miss, or _____ ?

B   Ms.

A   Thank you. Have a nice day.

B   Thanks. You too.

2 Your personal information

Vocabulary | Complete the form. Use your own information.

Touchstone English Club

NAME: _____

First   Middle   Last

☐ single   ☐ married

CLASS: _____

ROOM: _____

TEACHER: _____

3 Are we in the same class?

Grammar **A** Complete the conversation. Write *am* or *are*. Use contractions *'m* or *'re* where possible.

Receptionist Hello. ___Are___ you here for
an English class?

Mi-Young Yes, I _____ . I'm Mi-Young.

Receptionist Mi-Young Lee? You _____ in Class C.

Mi-Young Thank you.

Sergio Hi. _____ I in Class C, too? I'm Sergio.

Receptionist Yes, you _____ .

Sergio So we _____ in the same class.

Receptionist Wait. _____ you Sergio Rodrigues?

Sergio No, I _____ not. I'm Sergio Lopes.

Receptionist Oh, you _____ in Class D.
You _____ not in the same class.

B Complete the conversation.

David Hi. _____ _____ Julia Kim?

Leti No, _____ _____ . I'm Leticia Martinez,
but everyone calls me Leti.

David Hi, Leti. I'm David. Nice to meet you.

Leti _____ _____ here for a dance class?

David Yes, _____ _____ . _____ _____
in the same class?

Leti Yes, _____ _____ . We're in Class A.

4 About you

Grammar Answer the questions. Use your own information.

1. Are you in an English class?

   _____

2. Are you in a French class?

   _____

3. How are you today?

   _____

4. Are you and your friends in the same English class?

   _____

5. Are you married?

   _____

1 What's the number?

Vocabulary **A** Write the numbers.

0	1	2	3	4	5
zero	_____	_____	_____	_____	_____

	6	7	8	9	10
	_____	_____	_____	_____	_____

B Complete the crossword puzzle.

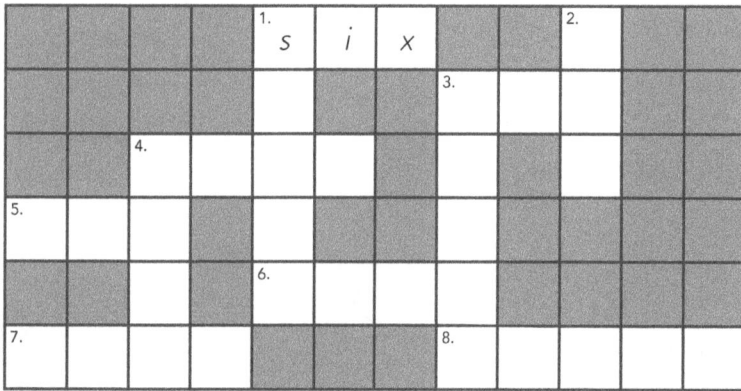

Across

1. two × three = ___six___

3. two + eight = _____

4. ten ÷ two = _____

5. six – four = _____

6. three + six = _____

7. five × zero = _____

8. six + two = _____

Down

1. ten – three = _____

2. eight – seven = _____

3. eight – five = _____

4. two × two = _____

2 What's the word?

Vocabulary The letters spell a word. Write each letter in the correct box below to see the word.

1. C	3. H	5. N	7. E	9. U
2. O	4. O	6. T	8. S	10. T

ten	four	nine	one	three	eight	six	two	five	seven
			C						

3 Here's your membership card.

Grammar | **Look at Mark's student ID card. Write his answers in the conversation.**

Lee   Hello. Are you a member of the club?

Mark   No, I'm not.

Lee   OK. Well, here's an application form.
So, what's your last name?

Mark   *It's Brokaw.* **or** *Brokaw.*
   or *My last name's Brokaw.*

Student ID Card
Mark A. Brokaw

Telephone: 740-555-2968
Email: mab@cup.org
Department: English (Mrs. Roberts)

Lee   Thank you. And your first name?

Mark   _____

Lee   What's your middle initial, please?

Mark   _____

Lee   And what's your email address?

Mark   _____

Lee   And your phone number?

Mark   _____

Lee   Are you an English student?

Mark   _____

Lee   What's your teacher's name?

Mark   _____

Lee   Thank you. Here's your membership card.
Have a nice day.

4 About you

Grammar and vocabulary | **Write questions with *What's* and the words given. Then answer the questions with your own information.**

1. A *What's your name?*
           (your name)

     B _____

2. A _____
          (your cell phone number)

     B _____

3. A _____
          (your email address)

     B _____

4. A _____
          (your English teacher's name)

     B _____

1 Good evening.

Conversation strategies Complete the conversations with the expressions in the box. Use each expression only one time.

| Good evening. | ✓ Hi | How about you? | How are you doing? | Thank you. | Yes |
| Pretty good. | Hello. | Nice to meet you. | Good-bye. | thanks. | Yeah |

1. Sam   Hi, Ali.

   Ali   ____Hi____ , Sam. _____

   Sam   Good, thanks. How about you?

   Ali   _____

   Sam   Am I late?

   Ali   _____ , you are, but it's OK.

   Sam   Good. By the way, here's your book.

   Ali   Oh, _____

2. Joe   Good evening.

   Clerk   _____ What's your name, please?

   Joe   Joe Johnson.

   Clerk   Oh, yes. Mr. Johnson. Your room number is
          10A. Here's your key.

   Joe   _____

3. Sally   Hello. My name's Sally.

   Kate   _____ I'm Kate. _____

         Are you here on business?

   Sally   _____ , I am. _____

   Kate   No, I'm on vacation.

   Sally   Nice. Oh, here's a taxi. _____

   Kate   Bye.

2 How are you doing?

A Rewrite the conversation. Use less formal expressions for the underlined words.

A <u>Hello. How are you?</u>

A *Hi. How are you doing?*

B <u>I'm fine, thank you.</u> How are you?

B _____

A <u>I'm fine.</u> Are you a student here?

A _____

B <u>Yes,</u> I am. How about you?

B _____

A <u>Yes,</u> me too.

A _____

B What's the email address here?

A It's goodschool1@cup.org.

B <u>Thank you. Good-bye.</u>

B _____

A <u>Good-bye.</u>

A _____

B Number the lines of the conversation in the correct order. Then write the conversation.

____ Hi.

A *Hello.*

____ Yeah, me too.

B _____

____ OK.

A _____

____ Are you here for the concert?

B _____

____ How are you doing?

A _____

1 Hello.

B _____

____ Yeah, I am. How about you?

A _____

Unit 1 Progress chart

What can you do? Mark the boxes. ☑ = I can . . . ? = I need to review how to . . .	To review, go back to these pages in the Student's Book.
☐ make statements with *I'm (not)*, *you're (not)*, and *we're (not)*.	2, 4, and 5
☐ ask questions with *Are you . . . ?*	5
☐ ask questions with *What's . . . ?*	4, 6, and 7
☐ give answers with *It's . . . .*	6 and 7
☐ say *hello* and *good-bye* in at least 4 different ways.	1, 2, and 3
☐ talk about names in English.	2 and 4
☐ use numbers 0–10.	6
☐ use *How about you?*	8
☐ use everyday expressions in more formal and less formal situations.	9

Grammar — *Vocabulary* — *Conversation strategies*

Where is everybody today?

Grammar | **A** Look at the pictures. Complete the sentences.

1. Bill _'s_____ at the gym.
   __He's___ not at home.

2. Jon and Karen ___are___ at
   home. _____ not in class.

3. Sun-Yee _____ in the
   cafeteria. _____ late.

4. David _____ on vacation.
   _____ asleep.

5. Kate and Tess _____ in
   class. _____ not at the
   library.

6. Carmen _____ at work.
   _____ not sick.

B Complete the questions about the people in part A. Then answer the questions.

1. A ___Is___ Bill at work?
   B _No, he's not._____

2. A _____ Jon and Karen at home?
   B _____

3. A _____ Sun-Yee at the gym?
   B _____

4. A _____ David asleep?
   B _____

5. A _____ Kate and Tess on vacation?
   B _____

6. A _____ Carmen at work?
   B _____

2 Absent classmates

Grammar **Complete the conversation with the verb *be*. Use contractions where possible. Add *not* where necessary.**

Silvia   Hi. How ___are___ you?

Jason   Good, thanks. How about you?

Silvia   Pretty good. _____ Dave here?

Jason   No, he _____ _____ .
I think he _____ sick.

Silvia   Oh. _____ he at home?

Jason   I don't know.

Silvia   How about Jenny and Paula?
_____ they here?

Jason   No, they _____ _____ . They _____
on vacation. I think they _____ in Miami.

Silvia   Look! Dave _____ not sick. He _____ over
there. He _____ just late again!

3 About you

Grammar
and
vocabulary **Complete the questions with the names of your friends and classmates. Then answer the questions.**

1. A Is ___Paul___ at home?
    B ___Yes, he is._____

2. A Are _____ and _____ at work?
    B _____

3. A Is _____ in class today?
    B _____

4. A Are _____ and _____ on vacation?
    B _____

5. A Are _____ and _____ in your English class?
    B _____

6. A Is _____ sick today?
    B _____

7. A Is _____ at the library?
    B _____

8. A Are _____ and _____ asleep?
    B _____

1 Everyday things

Vocabulary | Label the things in the pictures. Use *a* or *an* where necessary.

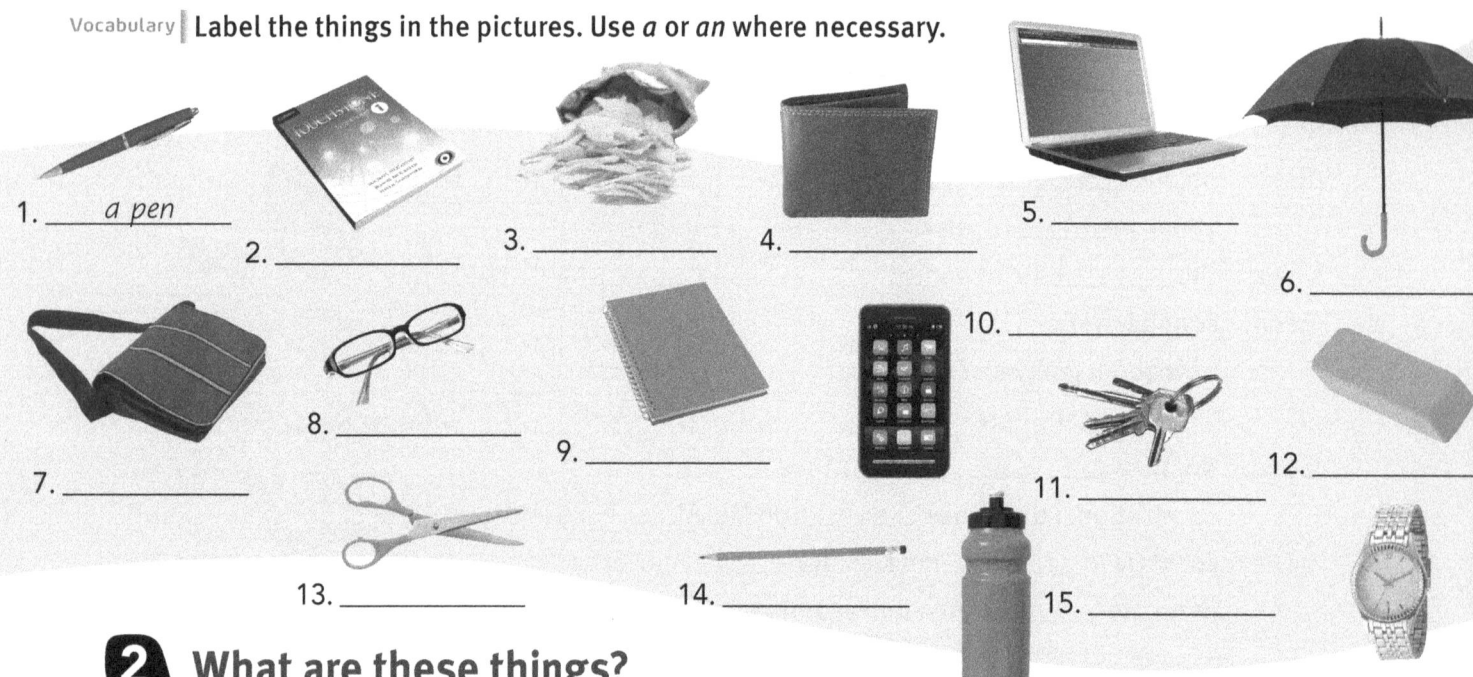

1. ___a pen___
2. _____
3. _____
4. _____
5. _____
6. _____
7. _____
8. _____
9. _____
10. _____
11. _____
12. _____
13. _____
14. _____
15. _____
16. _____

2 What are these things?

Grammar and vocabulary | Write sentences about the pictures.

1. ___This is a bag.___
2. ___These are pens.___
3. _____
4. _____

5. _____
6. _____
7. _____
8. _____

3 Asking about things

Complete the conversations. Use the words in the box.

Is	it	it's	these	they're	this	What
Is	it's	these	they	they're	this	✓What's

1.

Clerk	You're in Room 102.
Ms. Simms	Thanks. _*What's*_ this?
Clerk	Oh, _____ your room key.
Ms. Simms	OK. Thank you.
Clerk	And _____ is your membership card for the fitness club.

2.

Erica	What's _____ ? _____ it a smartphone?
Jim	No, _____ not. It's a GPS.
Erica	Oh.
Jim	_____ are these?
Erica	I think _____ watches.

3.

Bob	What are _____ ?
Jill	Oh, no! I think _____ my jeans.
Bob	Oh, I'm sorry. Are _____ new?
Jill	Yeah. Oh, look. _____ this your wallet?
Bob	Yes, _____ is.
Jill	Oh, no! And _____ are your credit cards!

1 Classroom things

Vocabulary | **A** Write the words under the pictures. Use *a* or *some*.

1. ___a board___

2. ___some posters___

3. _____

4. _____

5. _____

6. _____

7. _____

8. _____

9. _____

10. _____

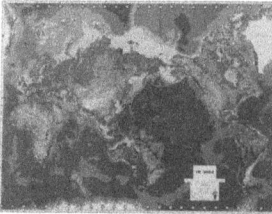

11. _____

12. _____

B Circle the words from part A in the puzzle. Look in these directions (→ ↓). Which word is *not* in the puzzle?

T	V	C	Q	U	A	B	L	A	M	A	B
W	E	H	A	S	I	P	U	Y	A	Z	O
A	C	A	L	E	N	D	A	R	P	H	A
G	O	I	H	K	O	B	Z	O	E	O	R
I	P	R	P	E	D	L	F	L	T	E	D
W	A	S	T	E	B	A	S	K	E	T	I
R	K	T	O	R	R	J	O	O	M	U	M
O	C	U	O	S	J	E	C	D	E	S	K
N	L	L	G	T	O	R	X	I	T	J	A
C	O	M	P	U	T	E	R	O	T	D	S
M	C	A	S	M	P	O	S	T	E	R	S
A	K	S	C	I	S	S	O	R	S	A	R

2 A classroom

Grammar and vocabulary | **A** Look at the picture. Complete the sentences. Use the words in the box.

in	in front of	in front of	next to	✓on	on	on	under

1. The workbooks are ___*on*___ the table.
2. The calendar is _____ the wastebasket.
3. The computer is _____ the teacher's desk.
4. The map is _____ the window.

5. The students' papers are _____ the wall.
6. The teacher's desk is _____ the board.
7. The scissors are _____ the teacher's desk.
8. The table is _____ the chairs.

B Write the questions about the classroom in part A.

1. A *Where's the teacher's desk?*
   B It's in front of the board.

2. A _____
   B It's next to the window.

3. A _____
   B They're on the table.

4. A _____
   B They're under the teacher's desk.

5. A _____
   B They're on the wall.

6. A _____
   B It's in the wastebasket.

3 Missing apostrophes

Grammar | Put apostrophes (') in the correct places in the questions. Then answer the questions.

1. What's on the wall in your classroom?   _____

2. What are your friends names?   _____

3. Whats your English teachers name?   _____

4. Wheres your teacher now?   _____

1 Questions, questions

Conversation
strategies Complete the conversations. Use the expressions in the box.

✓Excuse me	Thanks anyway.	Sure.	Here you go.	Thanks.
Can I borrow	You're welcome.	please	How do you spell	Sorry.
What's the word for this in English?				

1. Callie   _Excuse me_   , Bob.

   Bob   Yeah?

   Callie   _____ your English book?

   Bob   Sure. Now, where is it?

   Callie   Um . . . it's right in front of you.

   Bob   Oh, yeah. _____

   Callie   Thanks.

   Bob   _____

2. Ruby   Can I borrow your cell phone,

   _____ ?

   Millie   _____ Oh, wait.

   It's not in my bag. I think it's at home.

   _____

   Ruby   That's OK. _____

   Millie   Sure. . . . _____

   Ruby   In English, the word is _umbrella_.

   Millie   Umbrella? Thanks.

   Ruby   Sure.

3. Yuri   _____ _computers_?

   Dan   C-O-M-P-U-T-E-R-S.

   Yuri   _____

   Dan   Sure.

   Yuri   And how do you spell _television_?

   Dan   T-V.

   Yuri   Very funny!

2 Scrambled conversations

Number the lines of the conversations in the correct order. Then write the conversations.

1. _____ I'm sorry.   A _You're late._____

   ___1___ You're late.   B _____

   _____ That's OK.   A _____

2. _____ Sure.   A _____

   _____ Thank you.   B _____

   _____ Can I borrow your pen, please?   A _____

   _____ You're welcome.   B _____

3. _____ I don't know.   A _____

   _____ That's OK. Thanks anyway.   B _____

   _____ That's OK. What about this?   A _____

   _____ I'm sorry. I don't know.   B _____

   _____ What's the word for this?   A _____

Unit 2 Progress chart

What can you do? Mark the boxes. ☑ = I can . . . ? = I need to review how to . . .	To review, go back to these pages in the Student's Book.
☐ make statements with *he's (not)*, *she's (not)*, and *they're (not)*.	12 and 13
☐ ask questions with *Is he . . . ?*, *Is she . . . ?*, and *Are they . . . ?*	13
☐ use *a* or *an*.	14
☐ make nouns plural with *-s*, *-es*, or *-ies*.	15
☐ use *this* with singular nouns and *these* with plural nouns.	14 and 15
☐ ask questions with *Where . . . ?*	17
☐ use *'s* and *s'* to show possession.	17
☐ name at least 8 things students take to class.	14 and 15
☐ name at least 12 classroom items.	16 and 17
☐ say where things are in the classroom.	16 and 17
☐ ask for help in class.	18
☐ use common responses to *Thank you* and *I'm sorry*.	19

Grammar

Vocabulary

Conversation strategies

1 Favorites

Vocabulary | **A** Unscramble the letters. Write the words.

1. rgiens s_inger_

2. ctrao a_____

3. rtweir w_____

4. maet t_____

5. ralype p_____

6. dnab b_____

7. prsot s_____

8. naf f_____

9. ivome m_____

10. rtiats a_____

B Complete the crossword puzzle with the words in part A.

```
                              1.
            2.

        3.
            s  i  n  g  e  r
    4.                  5.        6.
7.
8.

                              9.
                      10.
```

Across

3. Adele is an amazing _____ .

5. Our favorite soccer _____ is Manchester United.

8. Hugh Jackman is a great _____ .

10. Ronaldo is a famous soccer _____ .

Down

1. Soccer is a _____ .

2. J.K. Rowling is a famous _____ .

4. Who's your favorite _____ ?

6. This _____ is exciting.

7. My favorite _____ is Coldplay.

9. Brian is a _____ of the Giants.

2 She's my favorite singer.

Grammar | **Look at the pictures. Complete the sentences.**

1. "_She's_ my favorite singer.
   Her new album is great."

2. "_____ Jama fans. Jama is
   _____ favorite band."

3. "_____ a great writer.
   _____ new book is really
   good."

4. "_____ favorite movie is
   The Aliens. What's _____
   favorite movie?"

5. "_____ my favorite actors.
   I think _____ movies are
   very good."

6. "Cassandra Coe is my teacher.
   _____ a great artist. _____
   pictures are amazing."

3 They're great!

Grammar | **Complete the conversation with the verb *be*. Use contractions where possible.**

Alicia I love this new Bruno Mars album. He _'s_ my favorite singer.

Norah Yeah. I _____ a big fan of his, too. His voice _____
        amazing. His songs _____ great.

Alicia Yeah. So, what's your favorite band?

Norah Maroon 5. They _____ great.

Alicia Yes, they _____ very talented. Adam Levine _____ really
        good looking. He _____ my favorite.

1   What are they like?

Vocabulary | Look at the pictures. Complete the sentences. Use the words in the box.

busy	fun	lazy	✓quiet	smart	tired
friendly	interesting	outgoing	shy	strict	

1. She's _____*quiet*_____ and _____ .

2. He's _____ .

3. They're _____ .

4. She's _____ .

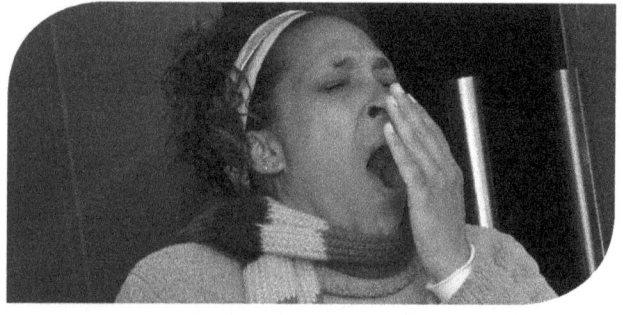

5. She's _____ .

6. He's _____ .

7. He's not very _____ or _____ .

8. They're _____ . She's _____ .

2 What's new?

Grammar | Complete the conversation with the verb *be*. Use contractions where possible. Add *not* where necessary.

Carrie Sorry. ___Am___ I late?

Josh No, you ____ _____ . You ____ fine.

Carrie Good. So, what's new? _____ you busy at work?

Josh Yes, I _____ . Our boss _____ sick, so he ____ _____ at work.

Carrie Oh, really?

Josh So, how about you? What _____ your new neighbors like? _____ they nice?

Carrie Yes, they _____ . They _____ OK. They _____ very quiet.

Josh _____ they students?

Carrie No, they ____ _____ . The guy _____ a writer.

Josh A writer? What about the woman? _____ she a writer, too?

Carrie No, she ____ _____ . She ____ _____ a writer – she _____ a teacher. At our school!

3 Make it negative.

Grammar | Rewrite the sentences in the negative form. Use contractions where possible.

1. My neighbors are very nice. *My neighbors aren't very nice.*
2. My best friend is a student. _____
3. I'm very shy. _____
4. The students in my class are very smart. _____
5. My English class is easy. _____
6. My teacher is very quiet. _____

4 About you

Grammar and vocabulary | Complete the questions. Then write short answers. Add more information.

1. ___Are___ you outgoing?   *Yes, I am. I'm very outgoing.*
   or   *No, I'm not. I'm not outgoing.*
2. _____ your best friend lazy? _____
3. _____ your English class hard? _____
4. _____ your friends smart? _____
5. _____ your teacher fun? _____
6. _____ your classmates nice? _____
7. _____ you tired today? _____
8. _____ you and your friends busy after class? _____

21

Lesson C   Family

1   Who's who?

Vocabulary | Use the family tree to complete the sentences about this family.

1. David is Paul's ___son___ .
2. John is Katy's _____ .
3. Katy is Paul's _____ .
4. Josh, David, and Emily are Paul and Katy's _____ .
5. Emily is Josh's _____ .
6. Josh is David's _____ .
7. John and Catherine are Katy's _____ .
8. Katy is Josh's _____ .
9. John is Catherine's _____ .
10. Emily is Katy's _____ .
11. Catherine is David's _____ .
12. John is Emily's _____ .
13. Susan is David's _____ .
14. Bill is Josh's _____ .
15. Robert is Emily's _____ .

2   What's the number?

Vocabulary | Write the numbers.

65
1. ___sixty-five___

11
2. _____

24
3. _____

15
4. _____

16
5. _____

91
6. _____

56
7. _____

77
8. _____

3 How about your children?

Grammar and vocabulary **Complete the conversations. Write the full questions.**

1. A How / your parents?

   How are your parents?

   B They're fine. Thanks. How / your mom?

   _____

   A She's good. She's on vacation right now.

2. A What / your sisters' names?

   _____

   B Beth and Kate. My brother's name is Pete.

   A Pete? Oh, how old / he?

   _____

   B He's 21.

3. A Who / this?

   _____

   B Oh, it's my aunt.

4. A My cousins are really fun.

   B Yeah? How old / they?

   _____

   A They're my age.

5. A Where / your family today?

   _____

   B At home. How about your family?

   A They're at home, too.

6. A Where / you from?

   _____

   B Well, my parents are from Italy originally.

   A Really? Where / your parents from in Italy?

   _____

   B They're from Rome.

4 A famous family

Grammar **Read part of a phone interview with an actor. Then write questions for the answers.**

Interviewer	Hello, Kate. How are you?
Kate	Hi. I'm fine, thanks.
Interviewer	Kate, I love your movies.
Kate	Thank you.
Interviewer	Now, about your family . . . who's your mother?
Kate	Gwen Russell – the artist. And Kevin Russell is my father.
Interviewer	Yes, they're famous! What are your parents like at home?
Kate	Oh, Dad's fun and outgoing. And Mom's very smart!
Interviewer	And, Kate, what's your favorite band?
Kate	Imagine Dragons. They're amazing. . . .

1. *How is Kate?*_____

   She's fine.

2. _____

   Her mother is Gwen Russell.

3. _____

   Her father is fun and outgoing. Her mother is very smart.

4. _____

   Her favorite band is Imagine Dragons.

Lesson D / A songwriter? Really?

1 New neighbors and co-workers

Conversation strategies | Complete the conversations with the questions in the box.

| How old is she? | Where is she from? | ✓What are they like? | An actor? Is she good? |
| From Chile? | Are they friendly? | Are they good? | Where are they from? |

1. **Ming**   Who are they?

   Jim   Oh, they're my new neighbors.

   Ming   Your neighbors? *What are they like?*

   Jim   Interesting. Very interesting. They're in a rock band.

   Ming   A rock band? _____

   Jim   They're from New York.

   Ming   Wow! _____

   Jim   No, they're not.

   Ming   Uh-oh. _____

   Jim   Oh, very. Their friends are always here!

2. **Carlos**   Who's she?

   Kim   Her name's Angie.

   Carlos   Angie? _____

   Kim   I don't know exactly. I think she's from Chile.

   Carlos   _____ Really?

   What's she like?

   Kim   She's outgoing and fun.

   Carlos   Really? _____

   Kim   I'm not sure. Maybe 24 or 25.

   Carlos   Oh. What's her job? Is she a server here?

   Kim   Well, yes. But she's an actor, too.

   Carlos   _____

   Kim   Yeah, she's a good actor but not a great server.

24

2 Really? I'm surprised!

Write responses to show you are interested or surprised. Then ask a question.

1. My grandmother's name is Banu.   _Really? What's she like?_

2. My brother is a singer in a band.

3. My grandfather is a tennis player.

4. I'm from Alaska.

5. My mother is a Spanish teacher.

6. My new job is hard work.

7. My sister is an artist.

8. My last name is Oh.

Unit 3 Progress chart

What can you do? Mark the boxes. ☑ = I can . . . ? = I need to review how to . . .	To review, go back to these pages in the Student's Book.
Grammar	
☐ use *my*, *your*, *his*, *her*, *our*, and *their*.	22 and 23
☐ make statements with *be*.	22 and 23
☐ ask *yes-no* questions with *be*.	24 and 25
☐ make negative statements with *be*.	24 and 25
☐ ask information questions with *be*.	26 and 27
Vocabulary	
☐ name at least 8 words to describe people's personalities.	24 and 25
☐ name at least 12 family words.	26 and 27
☐ say numbers 10–101.	26
Conversation strategies	
☐ show interest by repeating information and asking questions.	28
☐ use *Really?* to show interest or surprise.	29

Everyday life

Lesson A — In the morning

 1 **What's Kathy's morning like?**

Grammar and vocabulary

A Complete the sentences about Kathy's morning. Use the correct form of the verbs in the box.

check	exercise	✓get up	play
eat	get up	listen	read

1. Kathy ___gets up___ early. Her son _____ late.

2. She _____ before work. Her son _____ games.

3. She _____ to the radio in the car.

4. She and her co-workers _____ breakfast together.

5. Kathy _____ her email right after breakfast.

6. Her boss _____ the newspaper at work.

B Rewrite the sentences in the negative form. Use contractions where possible.

1. Kathy's son gets up early. _Kathy's son doesn't get up early._____

2. Kathy checks her email before breakfast. _____

3. Kathy and her son talk a lot in the morning. _____

4. Kathy's son does his homework. _____

5. Kathy and her boss eat breakfast together. _____

6. Kathy's boss plays computer games. _____

2 Guess what!

Grammar | Complete Peter's email with the correct form of the verbs.

> **New Message**
>
> To: Samir22@cup.com
> From: PeterJ@cup.com
> Subject: New Job
>
> Hi!
>
> Guess what! I ___*have*___ (have) a new job – in a coffee shop. It's hard work. I _____ (get up) early, and I _____ (work) late. But the coffee is good.
>
> My boss is nice. He's French, and he _____ (study) English at night. He _____ (do) his homework in the coffee shop. I _____ (help) him sometimes. He's quiet, and he _____ (not / talk) a lot. He _____ (listen) to the radio and _____ (sing), but we _____ (not / like) the same music. He _____ (like) coffee, too. We both _____ (have) four cups of coffee every day!
>
> Write soon!
>
> Peter

3 Typical morning activities

Grammar and vocabulary | **A** What are typical morning activities? Match the verbs with the words and expressions.

1. do __d__
2. study ____
3. check ____
4. listen ____
5. drive ____
6. play ____
7. read ____
8. go ____

a. to the radio
b. (my) email or messages
c. a car
✓d. (my) homework
e. on the Internet
f. English
g. games on the computer
h. a book

B Write true sentences about your morning routine. Use the verbs in part A.

1. *I don't do my homework in the morning.*
2. _____
3. _____
4. _____
5. _____
6. _____
7. _____
8. _____

1 What's fun? What's not?

A Which routine activities are fun for you? Complete the charts. Add your own ideas.

check email	do the laundry	go shopping	take a class
clean the house	eat snacks	make phone calls	text friends
do homework	get up early	✓ play sports	watch TV

Fun!	
play sports	

Not fun!	

B Write the days of the week in the date book. Then write one thing you do each day.

S *unday* : *I go shopping on Sundays.*   **Th**_____ : _____

M_____ : _____   **F**_____ : _____

T_____ : _____   **S**_____ : _____

W_____ : _____

2 About you 1

Use time expressions to write one thing you do and one thing you don't do.

1. on the weekends   *I clean the house on the weekends.*
   I don't go to work on the weekends.

2. after work / class   _____

3. every day   _____

4. on Saturdays   _____

5. in the afternoons   _____

6. at night   _____

3 What's your week like?

Grammar | **Complete the conversation with the correct form of the verbs.**

Cecilia   What's your week like, Eduardo? __Do__ (Do / Does) you __go__ (go / goes) to work every day?

Eduardo   Well, no, I _____ (don't / doesn't). I work at home on Fridays.

Cecilia   Really? What about on the weekends? _____ (Do / Does) you _____ (work / works) then, too?

Eduardo   Yes, I _____ (do / does). But I don't like it. What about you? _____ (Do / Does) you and your husband _____ (go / goes) to work every day?

Cecilia   Yes, we _____ (do / does). But just Monday to Friday. We _____ (clean / cleans) the house on the weekends. Oh, and we _____ (go / goes) to soccer games.

Eduardo   Oh. _____ (Do / Does) your son _____ (play / plays) soccer?

Cecilia   Yes, he _____ (do / does). He's on the school team. _____ (Do / Does) your son _____ (play / plays) any sports?

Eduardo   No, he _____ (don't / doesn't). He plays games on his computer.

4 About you 2

Grammar and vocabulary | **Complete the questions. Then write answers with your own information.**

1. A __Do__ you __take__ a class at night?
   B _Yes, I do. I take a Spanish class on Monday evenings._

2. A _____ your father _____ the laundry on weekends?
   B _____

3. A _____ you and your friends _____ shopping on Saturdays?
   B _____

4. A _____ your friends _____ their email before breakfast?
   B _____

5. A _____ your mother _____ the news on the Internet every day?
   B _____

Lesson C — Do you work out every day?

1 Saying more than *yes* or *no*

Conversation strategies **A** Complete the conversation. Use the sentences in the box.

> I work part-time in the cafeteria.   It's fun, and the people are nice.
> Just Mondays and Wednesdays.   I'm an English student.
> ✓ I'm new here, and I'm late.   I go there Mondays after work. It's great!

Mike   Hi. Are you OK? You look lost.

Yumi   Hello. Where's Room 106? Do you know?
   I'm new here, and I'm late.

Mike   Yeah. It's right over there, next to the cafeteria.

Yumi   Thanks. So, do you work here?

Mike   Yes, I do. _____

Yumi   Do you like the job?

Mike   Yeah, I do. _____

Yumi   That's good. Do you work here every day?

Mike   Well, no. _____

   I go to class on Tuesdays and Thursdays.

Yumi   Oh. So you're a student, too?

Mike   Yeah. _____

Yumi   Really? I'm an English student, too. Do you belong
to the English Club?

Mike   Yes, I do. _____

Yumi   Oh. Well, thanks a lot. And see you at English Club!

Mike   Great!

B Read the completed conversation again. Then read the sentences below.
Check (✓) *T* (true) or *F* (false).

	T	F
1. Mike and Yumi are friends.	☐	✓
2. Mike works in the cafeteria.	☐	☐
3. Mike is a new student.	☐	☐
4. Mike works Tuesdays and Thursdays.	☐	☐
5. Mike likes his part-time job.	☐	☐
6. Yumi and Mike are English students.	☐	☐
7. Mike belongs to the English Club.	☐	☐

30

2 About you

Conversation
strategies **Unscramble the questions. Then answer the questions. Write more than**
yes or no. Use *Well* if you need to.

1. live / you / around / Do / here ?

   Do you live around here?

2. from / originally / you / here / Are ?

3. a / full-time / you / Are / student ?

4. have / you / brothers / Do / sisters / or ?

5. you / work / the / on / weekends / Do ?

6. Do / your / every day / text / friends / you ?

7. get up / day / you / Do / every / early ?

8. grandparents / Do / with / your / live / you ?

Watching TV

Reading **A** What do you think average Americans do after work and school?
Check (✓) three boxes.

☐ spend time with family ☐ read ☐ watch TV
☐ go out with friends ☐ go out to dinner ☐ go shopping

B Read the article. Check your answers in part A.

After WORK and SCHOOL

Do Americans go out every night after work and have fun? Maybe the answer is surprising, but no, they don't. They don't usually go out with friends in the evening, and they don't go out to dinner or go shopping. So what do they do? Well, about 90% of Americans stay at home in the evening to relax. In fact, it's their favorite activity. They read, watch TV, and spend time with their families.

So what about young people? Well, they spend a lot of time at home, too. American high school students study about six hours a week and watch TV for about 15 hours a week.

Most Americans also have a hobby and do fun, interesting things like play sports or music. Americans stay home a lot, but they stay busy, too!

Here are average Americans' favorite activities:
• reading
• watching TV
• spending time with their families
• exercising
• using the Internet

C Read the article again. Then correct these false sentences.

1. Americans go out with friends every night after work.
   Americans don't usually go out with friends in the evening.

2. After work, Americans usually go shopping.
   _____

3. American high school students usually study for three hours a night.
   _____

4. American high school students don't watch TV.
   _____

5. The average American doesn't have a hobby.
   _____

2 Weekends

Writing **A** Read the email messages. Then rewrite Joe's message. Use capital letters and periods.

> **New Message** 🗕 🗗 ✕
>
> Hi Joe,
> Are you busy on weekends?
> I am. On Friday nights, I go to
> a club in Miami. On
> Saturdays, I sleep late. In the
> evening, I watch TV. On
> Sundays, I study. Do you
> study on the weekends?
> Ian

> **New Message** 🗕 🗗 ✕
>
> hi ian,
> yes, i have busy weekends on
> friday nights, i visit my family
> downtown on saturdays,
> i take a spanish class at grove
> college on sundays, i play
> soccer i don't study on
> weekends – i don't have time
> joe

> **New Message** 🗕 🗗 ✕
>
> *Hi Ian,*
> _____
> _____
> _____
> _____
> _____
> _____
> _____
> _____

B What do you do on weekends? Write an email to a friend about your weekend activities.

> **New Message** 🗕 🗗 ✕
>
> Hi _____ ,
> _____
> _____
> _____
> _____
> _____
> _____
> _____

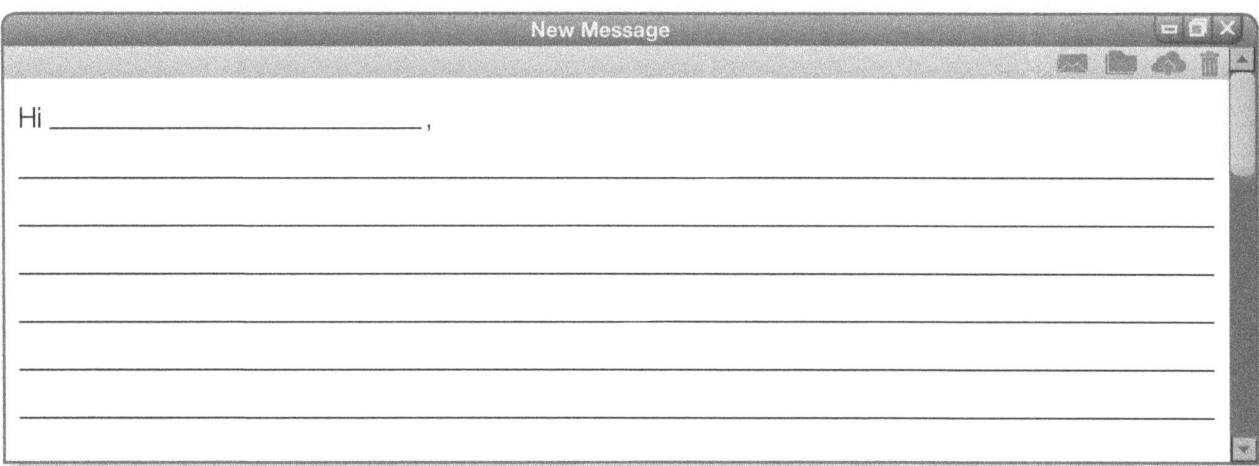

Unit 4 Progress chart

What can you do? Mark the boxes. ✓ = I can . . . ? = I need to review how to . . .	To review, go back to these pages in the Student's Book.
Grammar	
☐ make simple present statements.	34 and 35
☐ ask simple present *yes-no* questions and give short answers.	36 and 37
Vocabulary	
☐ name at least 12 new verbs for routine activities.	34, 35, 36, and 37
☐ name the days of the week.	36
☐ name at least 8 time expressions with the simple present.	37
Conversation strategies	
☐ answer questions with more than *yes* or *no*.	38 and 39
☐ use *Well* to get time to think of an answer.	39
Writing	
☐ use capital letters and periods.	41

1 In your free time

Vocabulary | How often do you do these things? Complete the chart with the free-time activities in the box. Add your own ideas.

| ✓ eat out | go out with friends | go to a club | go to the gym | play a sport |
| go on the Internet | go shopping | go to a movie | have dinner with family | text family |

every day	three or four times a week	once or twice a week	once or twice a month
		eat out	

2 Craig's busy schedule

Grammar and vocabulary | **A** Read Craig's weekly planner. Are the sentences below true or false? Write *T* (true) or *F* (false). Then correct the false sentences.

WEEKLY PLANNER

SUNDAY	MONDAY	TUESDAY	WEDNESDAY	THURSDAY	FRIDAY	SATURDAY
5	**6**	**7**	**8**	**9**	**10**	**11**
morning: *do the laundry!!*	morning: *classes*	morning: *go to the gym!*	morning: *classes*	morning: *go to the gym!*	morning: *classes*	morning: *clean the house!!*
	afternoon: *go shopping*	afternoon: *library*	afternoon: *guitar lesson*			afternoon: *tennis with Bob*
evening: *dinner with Mom and Dad*				evening: *dinner with Sandra*	evening: *movie with Jim*	evening: *club with Bill*

three evenings a week

1. He goes out with friends ~~every evening~~. __*F*__

2. He goes to the library every day. _____

3. He goes shopping once a week. _____

4. He takes guitar lessons on Wednesday mornings. _____

5. He plays tennis twice a week. _____

6. He does the laundry three times a week. _____

7. He sees his parents on the weekends. _____

8. He cleans the house on Saturday mornings. _____

Grammar **B** Now answer these questions about Craig's schedule.

1. How often does he go to the gym? *He goes to the gym twice a week.*
2. When does he have classes? _____
3. How often does he go to a club? _____
4. What does he do on Thursday evenings? _____
5. When does he go to the movies? _____
6. What does he do on Saturday afternoons? _____
7. Who does he play tennis with? _____
8. Where does he go on Saturday evenings? _____

3 About you

Grammar and vocabulary | **Write questions for a friend. Then answer your friend's questions.**

1. You *Where do you go after class?*
   (go after class)

   Friend I meet some friends and go to a restaurant for dinner.
   How about you?

   You _____

2. You _____
   (text your friends)

   Friend Every day. But I don't text before breakfast. How about you?

   You _____

3. You _____
   (do in your free time at home)

   Friend I rent a movie, or I just relax in front of the TV with a friend.
   How about you?

   You _____

4. You _____
   (go on the weekends)

   Friend I go to a restaurant or club. How about you?

   You _____

5. You _____
   (go out with)

   Friend Oh, friends from school. How about you?

   You _____

Lesson B / TV shows

1 How often?

Grammar **A** Write the frequency adverbs in order in the chart below.

✓always   hardly ever   never   often   sometimes   usually

| *always* | | | | | |

100%   0%

B Answer the questions. Write true sentences using frequency adverbs.

What's something you . . .

1. hardly ever do before school or work?   *I hardly ever check my email before school.*
2. always do in the morning?
3. sometimes do after school or work?
4. never do during dinner?
5. often do in the evening?
6. usually do on Saturdays?

2 What kinds of TV shows do you know?

Vocabulary **A** Look at the pictures. Circle the correct type of TV show.

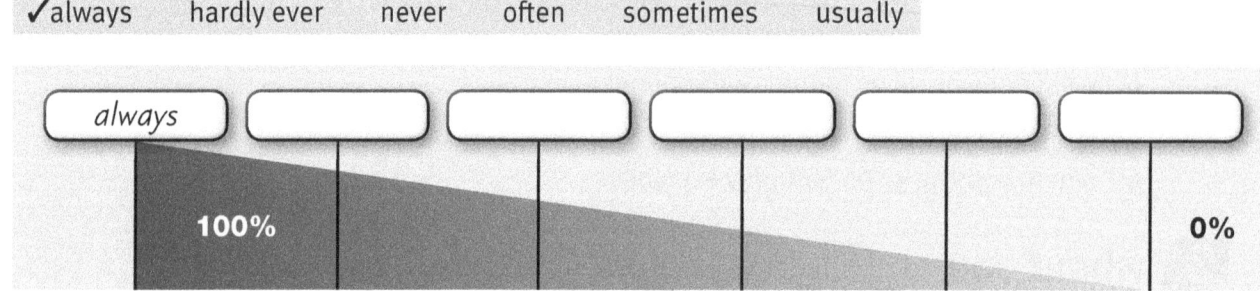

1. soap opera /
   the news
2. talk show /
   cartoon
3. sitcom /
   the news
4. cartoon /
   game show

5. documentary /
   talk show
6. talk show /
   cartoon
7. sitcom /
   reality show
8. the news /
   game show

B Circle the kinds of TV shows from part A in the puzzle. Look in these directions (→ ↓).

T	C	S	I	T	C	O	M	E	T	I	S
E	A	O	E	D	H	P	O	R	H	I	H
L	R	E	A	L	I	T	Y	S	H	O	W
K	T	A	L	K	S	H	O	W	U	P	O
S	O	A	P	O	P	E	R	A	E	E	U
D	O	C	U	M	E	N	T	A	R	Y	N
A	N	O	O	T	H	E	J	E	I	W	S
Y	T	E	A	I	U	W	D	O	C	T	V
Y	C	G	A	M	E	S	H	O	W	L	Y

3 About you

Grammar and vocabulary

Answer the questions. Give two pieces of your own information in each answer.

1. Do you ever watch soap operas? _Yes, I usually watch soap operas in the afternoons._
   I love the stories.

2. What sitcoms do you hardly ever watch? _____

3. How often do you watch documentaries? _____

4. What talk shows do you like? _____

5. When do you usually watch the news? _____

6. How often do you watch reality shows? _____

1 Asking questions in two ways

Conversation strategies | Complete the conversations with the questions in the box.

Do you like French?	I mean, do you belong to any clubs?
✓ Do you do anything special?	I mean, do you know a nice place?
Do you play baseball?	I mean, do you go every day?

1. Lisa   What do you do after work?
   Do you do anything special?

   Debbie   Well, I go to the gym.

   Lisa   Really? How often do you go?
   _____

   Debbie   No, not every day. I go Mondays, Wednesdays, and Thursdays.

2. Howard   Do you know the restaurants around here?
   _____

   Mary   Well, I often go to a little place on Main Street. What kind of food do you like?
   _____

   Howard   Yes, I do. I love French food.

3. Paul   What do you do after school?
   _____

   Tom   Well, yeah. I'm in the Sports Club.
   Paul   Really? What do you play?
   _____

   Tom   Well, no. We watch baseball on TV!
   Paul   Oh.

2 Questions, questions

Write a second question for each question below. Then write true answers.

1. What's your teacher like?
   I mean, is she nice?

   Yes, she's very nice. She's friendly.

2. How often do you have English class?

3. How do you get to school / work?

4. What do you do for fun on the weekends?

5. Do you read a lot?

6. Do you ever go to clubs?

3 About you

Add frequency adverbs to make these sentences true for you.
Then use *I mean*, and write more information.

1. I ___never___ go to the gym. *I mean, I usually exercise at home.*

2. I _____ get home early. _____

3. I _____ see my friends during the week. _____

4. I _____ go on the Internet in the evening. _____

5. I _____ eat breakfast at school / work. _____

6. I _____ get up early. _____

7. I _____ eat out on Saturdays. _____

8. I _____ watch reality shows on TV. _____

9. I _____ go shopping on the weekends. _____

10. I _____ study English after dinner. _____

1 Paula's problem

Reading **A** Read Paula's post to an online forum. How many hours does Paula spend online?

☐ 3 or 4 hours   ☐ 4 or 5 hours   ☐ 8 or 9 hours

PaulaT18   posted 2 hours ago

I live with my parents and my two brothers. They say I hardly ever spend time with them. My parents say I spend too much time on my phone and in front of my computer, but I don't think that's true. I mean, I often get up early and check my messages, but we always eat breakfast together. I guess I sometimes text during breakfast, but I never call people then. After class, I listen to music on my phone, but I also do my homework. In the evening, I often log on to my social network to chat with friends. They're always online. Sometimes I watch a movie on my computer. I usually spend eight or nine hours online every day. I don't think it's a problem. What do you think?

B Read Paula's post again. Then answer the questions.

1. Who does Paula live with? _She lives with her parents and her_
   two brothers.

2. Is she a student? _____
   _____

3. When does she log on to her social network? _____

4. What does Paula use her phone and computer for? _____
   _____
   _____

5. What do you think? Does Paula have a problem? Why or why not?
   _____
   _____
   _____

2 I need some advice!

Writing **A Read José's post to an online forum. Complete it with *and* or *but*.**

José   posted 2 hours ago

I think I have a problem. I don't have a computer at home, ___*but*___ I use a computer at
school. I usually go to school early, _____ I check my email. I send email to my friends in
other countries. I often go online for fun, _____ sometimes I study English on the computer.
Then on the weekends, I go to school _____ write papers for class (on the computer). Do I
spend too much time at school?

**B Write a post for an online forum about a problem you have. Write about a problem below,
or use your own idea.**

"I watch too much TV."   "I go shopping too much."   "I work too much."

"I stay home too much."   "I talk on my cell phone too much."   "I study too much."

_____
_____
_____
_____
_____
_____

Unit 5 Progress chart

What can you do? Mark the boxes. ✓ = I can . . . ? = I need to review how to . . .	To review, go back to these pages in the Student's Book.
Grammar	
ask simple present information questions.	44 and 45
use time expressions like *once a week*.	44 and 45
use frequency adverbs like *sometimes*, *never*, etc.	46
Vocabulary	
name at least 6 new free-time activities.	44 and 45
name at least 6 kinds of TV shows.	47
talk about likes and dislikes.	47
Conversation strategies	
ask questions in 2 ways to be less direct.	48
use *I mean* to repeat an idea and say more.	49
Writing	
use *and* and *but* to link ideas.	51

Neighborhoods

Lesson A / Nice places

1 **What's in the neighborhood?**

Vocabulary | Label the places in the picture. Use the words in the box with *a / an* or *some*.

✓apartment buildings	fast-food places	museum	park	restaurants	supermarket
club	movie theater	outdoor café	post office	stores	swimming pool

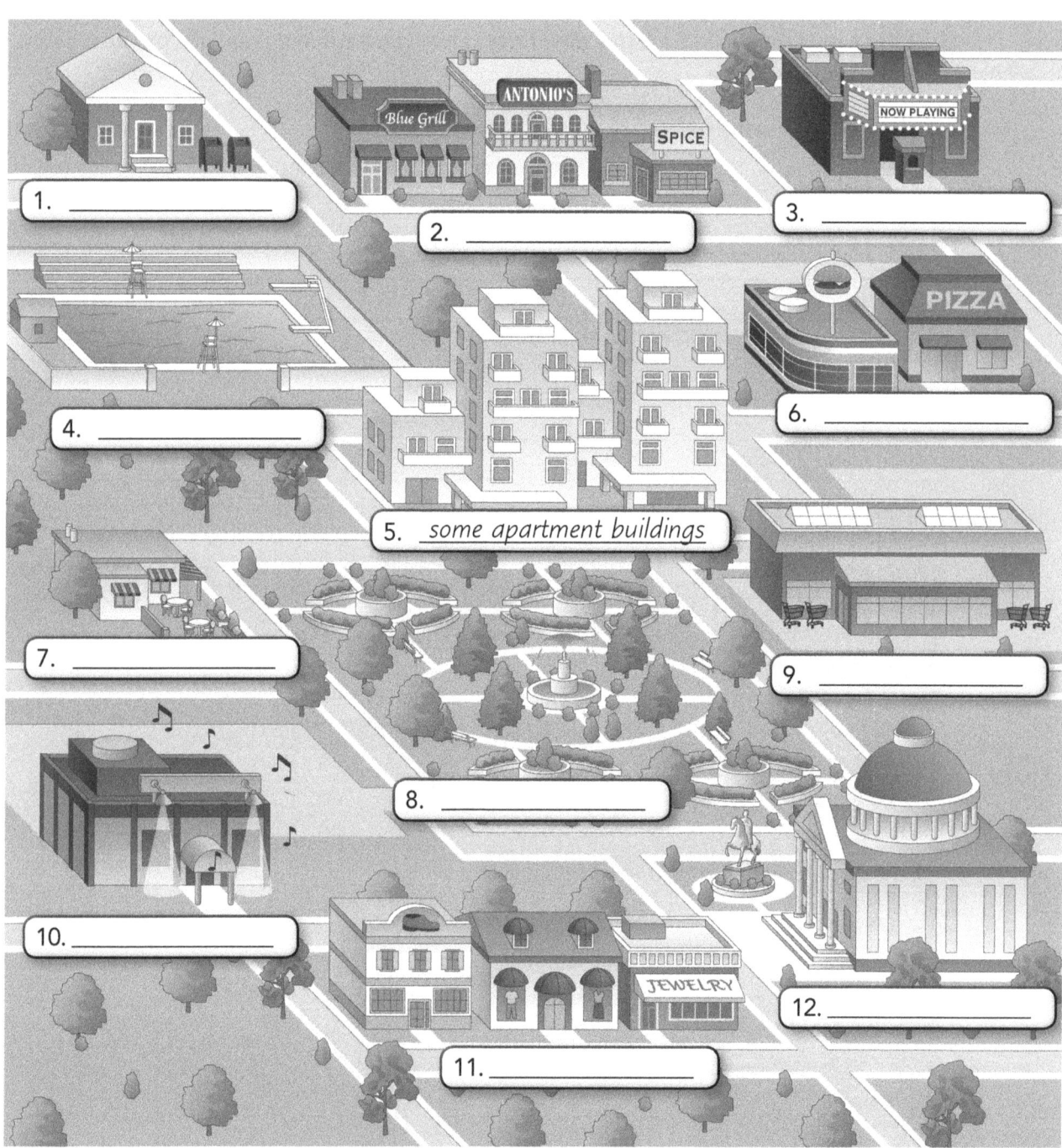

1. _____

2. _____

3. _____

4. _____

5. *some apartment buildings*

6. _____

7. _____

8. _____

9. _____

10. _____

11. _____

12. _____

2 Can you find the opposites?

Vocabulary Find six pairs of adjective opposites in the box. Write them in the chart below.

bad	boring	expensive	interesting	noisy	quiet
big	cheap	good	✓new	✓old	small

new – old

3 That's not quite right!

Grammar Look at the picture on page 42. Correct the sentences to describe the neighborhood.

1. There's one cheap fast-food place.   *There are a couple of cheap fast-food places.*
2. There are a couple of post offices.   _____
3. There's a big stadium.   _____
4. There are a couple of supermarkets.   _____
5. There are some malls.   _____
6. There's an apartment building.   _____
7. There are no small stores.   _____
8. There's an expensive restaurant.   _____
9. There are a lot of beautiful parks.   _____
10. There's no movie theater.   _____

4 About you

Grammar and vocabulary What's your neighborhood like? Complete the sentences with true information.

1. There's a _____ .
2. There are a lot of _____ .
3. There are some _____ .
4. There are a couple of _____ .
5. There's no _____ .
6. There are no _____ .

Lesson B / What time is it?

1 What's the time?

Vocabulary **A** Write the times in words. Where there are two lines, write the times two ways.

1. _It's twelve p.m._
   It's noon.

2. _____
   _____

3. _____

4. _____

5. _____
   _____

6. _____
   _____

B Read about Kayo's day. Write the times in numbers. Then number the sentences in the correct order.

_____ Her bus comes at __7:55__ (five to eight).

_____ She gets home at _____ (nine fifteen) and watches TV.

_1_ Kayo gets up at _____ (six twenty-five).

_____ She goes for lunch with her co-workers at _____ (noon).

_____ She starts work at _____ (eight forty-five).

_____ She meets her boyfriend at _____ (twenty five to six), and they have dinner.

_____ She eats breakfast at _____ (twenty after seven).

_____ She leaves work at _____ (ten after five).

_____ She goes to bed at _____ (ten thirty).

2 Let's do it!

Grammar | **Complete the conversations. Write questions starting with *What time . . . ?*
Use *Let's* to end each conversation with a suggestion.**

1. A I'm starving. Let's go to Burger Queen.
   B But it's late. *What time does it close?*
   A It closes around 11:00, I think. _____
   B Almost 10:00. _____

2. A There's a new reality show on TV tonight.
   B _____
   A Um, I think it starts at 8:00.
   B Well, I'm really tired. _____
   A I'm not sure. I think it ends at 9:30.
   B OK. _____

3. A Let's go to the gym on Saturday morning.
   B Sure. _____
   A Oh, it opens early. At 6:00. _____
   B I usually get up around 8:00 on Saturdays.
   A OK. _____

3 About you

Grammar and vocabulary | **Unscramble the questions. Then write true answers.**

1. do / What time / get up / on weekdays / you ?
   A *What time do you get up on weekdays?*
   B _____

2. your family / have / What time / does / lunch / on Sundays ?
   A _____
   B _____

3. your English class / What time / start / does ?
   A _____
   B _____

4. What time / leave home / do / you / in the morning ?
   A _____
   B _____

5. stores / do / What time / in your neighborhood / open and close ?
   A _____
   B _____

1 Responses

Conversation strategies **Circle the two correct responses to each comment. Cross out the incorrect response.**

1. I think every neighborhood needs a park.
   a. ~~Me neither.~~
   b. (Me too.)
   c. (Right.)

2. We don't have a good fast-food place here.
   a. Yeah.
   b. Me too.
   c. I know.

3. I don't like the new restaurant.
   a. Yeah. I know.
   b. Me neither.
   c. Me too.

4. There are no good bookstores around here.
   a. I know.
   b. Me too.
   c. Right.

5. I like the new outdoor café downtown.
   a. Me neither.
   b. Me too.
   c. Right. It's good.

6. I love this neighborhood. It's so quiet.
   a. Right.
   b. Yeah, I know.
   c. Me neither.

2 What do they have in common?

Conversation strategies **Read the conversation. Are the sentences below true or false? Write *T* (true) or *F* (false).**

Glen What's your new neighborhood like?

Anna Oh, it's amazing. There are a lot of outdoor cafés and movie theaters and clubs. I go out a lot.

Glen Really? I hardly ever go out in my neighborhood. It's boring.

Anna Let's do something in my neighborhood this weekend. I'm free on Saturday.

Glen Me too.

Anna Well, there's a great jazz club near my apartment. I love jazz.

Glen Really? Me too!

Anna But let's have dinner at a café first. The food at the club is expensive, and I don't have a lot of money.

Glen Me neither. So, let's meet at 6:30 at your apartment.

1. Glen and Anna both like their neighborhoods. _F_

2. Glen and Anna both go out a lot in their neighborhoods. _____

3. Glen and Anna are both free on Saturday. _____

4. Glen and Anna both love jazz. _____

5. Glen and Anna both have a lot of money. _____

> ✎ **Help note**
>
> *Glen and Anna **both** love jazz.*
> *Glen loves jazz, **and** Anna loves jazz, **too**.*

3 Right. I know.

Circle the expression that is true about your neighborhood. Then show you agree. Respond with *Right* or *I know*.

1. A (There are some) / There are no good restaurants in my neighborhood.
   B *I know.*

2. A My neighborhood **has** / **doesn't have** a lot of great stores.
   B _____

3. A I live in a **great** / **terrible** neighborhood.
   B _____

4. A We **need** / **don't need** a shopping mall around here.
   B _____

4 About you

Imagine you're talking to people from your neighborhood. Write true responses.

1. I really like this neighborhood.
   Me too. I think it's great.
   or
   Really? I don't like it very much.

2. I don't eat out in this neighborhood.
   _____

3. I think the restaurants are very expensive here.
   _____

4. I don't know a lot of people around here.
   _____

5. I think our neighborhood is boring.
   _____

6. I think we need a couple of new stores in our neighborhood.
   _____

A neighborhood guide

1 Free weekend events!

Reading | **A** Read about some local events on a website. Match the pictures with the events. Write the correct numbers next to the pictures.

Downtown Weekend Section

* * * FREE EVENTS * * *

1. All Day Music Meet local bands, singers, and musicians at City Park this Sunday. Listen to great music, dance to pop songs, or take a music workshop and write your own song! The music starts at 3 p.m. and finishes at 11 p.m. Call Melissa at 555-9075 for more information.

2. Spring Food Festival Do you love food? Do you often eat out? Then come to the Parkview Food Festival. Eat some delicious food from 20 different restaurants around the neighborhood – all for FREE! *Saturday from 11:00 a.m. to 4:00 p.m. at Green Street Park.*

3. Outdoor Street Fair *Saturday and Sunday from 10:00 a.m. to 6:00 p.m. in front of the City Art Museum.* There are a lot of beautiful items for sale – books, art, photos, paintings, clothes, and more. Items for sale are just $2–$25. Coffee, sodas, and snacks are for sale, too!

4. Free Classes at the Neighborhood Center Do you want to take a class but don't have the time? Try a free one-hour class Monday through Friday this week. Learn:
- Art
- Spanish
- Music
- French
- Computers
- Yoga

Classes start at 10:00 a.m. and 2:00 p.m. Go to www.freeclass.cup.org for more information.

B Read the website again. Then answer the questions. Check (✓) the correct events.

Which events . . .	The concert	The food festival	The street fair	The free classes
1. have food?	☐	☑	☑	☐
2. are on Saturday?	☐	☐	☐	☐
3. have a website?	☐	☐	☐	☐
4. are during the day?	☐	☐	☐	☐
5. are at night?	☐	☐	☐	☐
6. are outdoors?	☐	☐	☐	☐

2 Make your own event.

Writing **A** Complete the sentences with the prepositions in the box.

at	at	at	between	for	✓from	on	through	to

1. The event is __from__ 6:00 _____ 10:00.
2. The event is _____ 8:00 p.m. _____ the stadium _____ Main Street.
3. Go to www.eventinfo.cup.org _____ more information, or call Jim _____ 555-7777.
4. Call _____ 12:00 p.m. and 5:00 p.m., Monday _____ Friday.

B Imagine you are planning an event. Answer the questions. Use the ideas in the boxes and your own ideas.

Events:	Places:
a play, an art exhibit, a concert, a sports event	the library, the museum, the park, the theater

1. What is the event? _____
2. When and where is it? _____
3. What time does it start and finish? _____
4. What's the cost of the event? Is it free? _____
5. What things are there to do at the event? _____
6. Where or how do people get more information? _____

C Write an ad for an event in your town or city. Give the event a name.

_____
_____
_____

Unit 6 Progress chart

What can you do? Mark the boxes. ✓ = I can . . . ? = I need to review how to . . .	To review, go back to these pages in the Student's Book.
Grammar	
use *There's* and *There are* with singular and plural nouns.	54 and 55
use quantifiers *a lot of*, *some*, *a couple of*, and *no*.	54 and 55
use adjectives before nouns.	55
ask and answer questions about time.	56 and 57
make suggestions with *Let's*.	57
Vocabulary	
name at least 6 adjectives to describe places.	54 and 55
name at least 10 words for neighborhood places.	54 and 55
give times for events.	56 and 57
Conversation strategies	
answer *Me too* or *Me neither* to show I'm like someone.	58 and 59
answer *Right* or *I know* to agree.	59
Writing	
use prepositions *at*, *from*, *in*, *on*, and *to* with times, places, and days.	61

Out and about

Lesson A / Away for the weekend

1 **What's the weather like?**

Vocabulary **A** Write two sentences about each picture.

1. _It's hot._ _____ 2. _____ 3. _____
   It's sunny. _____   _____   _____

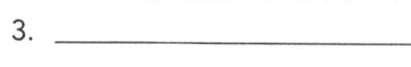

4. _____ 5. _____ 6. _____
   _____   _____   _____

B Answer the questions. Write true answers.

1. How many seasons do you have in your city? What are they? _____
   _____

2. What's your favorite season? Why? _____
   _____

3. What kind of weather do you like? Cold weather? Hot weather? _____
   _____

4. What's the weather like today? Is it warm? _____
   _____

5. What's the weather usually like at this time of year? _____
   _____

6. Does it ever snow in your city? If yes, when? _____
   _____

2 I'm waiting for a friend.

Grammar | Complete the conversation. Use the present continuous.

Erin Hi, Ken. It's Erin. Where are you?

Ken Oh, hi, Erin. I'm at the beach. I _'m spending_ (spend) the day with Tom. It's beautiful here today! It's, uh . . .

Erin Nice. . . . I'm so happy you _____ (have) fun.

Ken Yeah. We _____ (relax).
We _____ (not do) anything
special – I mean, I _____ (read)
a book, and Tom _____ (swim).
How about you? Are you at work?

Erin No. I _____ (not work) today.

Ken Oh, right. So, where – oops! Uh, I'm sorry.
I _____ (eat) ice cream. I'm starving.

Erin Yeah, me too. I _____ (eat) a cookie.

Ken Really? So, where are you? I mean, are you at home?

Erin No, I'm at Pierre's Café. I _____ (wait)
for a friend. He's very late.

Ken Oh, really? Who?

Erin You!

3 About you

Grammar and vocabulary | Are these sentences true or false for you right now? Write *T* (true) or *F* (false).
Then correct the false sentences.

1. _F_ I'm eating dinner right now.
    I'm not eating dinner right now. I'm doing my homework.

2. _____ I'm using a computer.
    _____

3. _____ My family is watching TV.
    _____

4. _____ My friends are working.
    _____

5. _____ It's snowing.
    _____

6. _____ My best friend is skiing.
    _____

1 All about sports

Vocabulary | **A** Write the names of the sports or kinds of exercise under the pictures.

1. _____volleyball_____

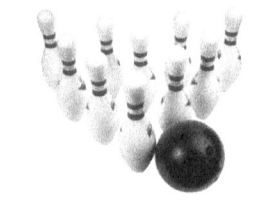

2. _____

3. _____

4. _____

5. _____

6. _____

7. _____

8. _____

9. _____

B Complete the chart with the words in part A.

People play . . .	People do . . .	People go . . .
volleyball		

C Answer the questions. Write true answers.

1. What sports do you play? How often? _I play volleyball on Wednesdays and_ _____
   basketball on the weekends. _____

2. What sports do your friends play? _____
   _____

3. Do you ever go biking? _____
   _____

4. What sports do people in your country like? _____
   _____

2 What are you doing?

Grammar | **Complete the conversations with present continuous questions.**

1. Joe   Hey, Luis! *What are you doing* (What / you / do) ?
   Are you at home?

   Luis   No, I'm at the park. I'm playing tennis.

   Joe   Really? _____ (you / play)
   with Janet?

   Luis   No, I'm playing with John today.

   Joe   Oh. So, _____ (you / have / fun) ?

   Luis   No, I'm not. You know, it's raining here, and it's cold.

   Joe   That's too bad. _____ (you / play)
   right now? In the rain?

   Luis   Yes, we are. And it's my turn to serve. Hold on a minute. . . .

   Joe   So, um, _____ (you / win) ?

   Luis   Uh, no. I'm not playing very well today.

   Joe   Is it because you're talking on your
   cell phone?

2. Janet Hi, Kelly. _____ (How / you / do) ?

   Kelly Hi. Great. How are you? _____ (you / work)
   this summer?

   Janet Yes, I'm working at a gym. I'm teaching there. It's fun.

   Kelly Really? _____ (What / you / teach) ?

   Janet Aerobics.

   Kelly Cool. So, _____ (you / do) other things?
   I mean, _____ (you / swim), too?

   Janet Yeah. There's a pool at the gym. So, _____
   (you / do) anything special this summer?

   Kelly Well, no. I'm living in my sister's apartment. She's in
   San Francisco this summer.

   Janet Really? _____ (What / she / do)
   there?

   Kelly She's working in a restaurant.

   Janet _____ (she / meet) a lot of
   new people?

   Kelly Oh, yes. She's having a good time.

Lesson C / How's it going?

1 Keep the conversation going!

Conversation strategies | Complete the conversation with the follow-up questions in the box.

Where are you working?   ✓ What are you doing?
Are you practicing your languages?   So, why are you studying Spanish and Portuguese?
What classes are you taking?   Are you enjoying your classes?

Alex   Hey, Kate. How's it going?

Kate   Good. How are things with you?

Alex   Great. But I'm really busy this summer.

Kate   Really? _What are you doing?_____

Alex   Well, I'm taking a couple of classes, and I'm working.

Kate   Wow! You're working and studying? _____

Alex   I'm taking Spanish and Portuguese.

Kate   That's interesting. _____

Alex   Yeah, I really am. I'm learning a lot!

Kate   That's great. _____

Alex   Well, I'm thinking about a trip to South America.

Kate   That's exciting!

Alex   Yeah, and that's why I'm working two jobs, you know.

Kate   Right. _____

Alex   Well, I'm working at a Peruvian restaurant from 11:00 to 5:00, and I'm working at a Brazilian music club at night.

Kate   Really? Wow! _____

Alex   Yes, I am! I'm speaking Spanish all day and Portuguese all night.

Kate   That's really cool! But when do you sleep?

Alex   That's a problem. Sometimes I sleep in class.

Kate   Oh, right. That *is* a problem.

54

2 Asking follow-up questions

Conversation strategies **Complete two follow-up questions for each comment.**

1. "I don't play sports, but I often go running with a friend."

   Really? Where _do you go running_ ?
   How often _____ ?

2. "My parents are on vacation this month."

   That's nice. Where _____ ?
   Are they _____ ?

3. "My grandparents are visiting this week."

   Really? Where _____ ?
   How often _____ ?

4. "I'm working nights this summer."

   Really? Where _____ ?
   What time _____ ?

3 Oh, that's good.

Conversation strategies **Read these people's comments about their summer activities. Complete the responses. Then ask follow-up questions.**

1. I'm really enjoying my vacation this summer.

   Oh, that's _good_ .
   What are you doing ?

2. I'm not doing anything exciting. I'm just reading a lot.

   That's _____ .
   _____ ?

3. I'm not enjoying this summer at all. I'm working ten hours a day.

   Really? That's _____ .
   _____ ?

4. I'm just relaxing, and I'm watching a lot of TV.

   Hey, that's _____ .
   _____ ?

5. I'm exercising a lot at the gym this summer.

   That's _____ .
   _____ ?

6. What vacation? I'm painting my house right now.

   Really? That's _____ .
   _____ ?

Lesson D Staying in shape

1 An advice column

Reading **A** Which sports and exercises do you do? Check (✓) the boxes.

☐ aerobics   ☐ biking   ☐ skiing   ☐ volleyball
☐ basketball   ☐ running   ☐ soccer   ☐ weight training

B Read the advice column. Match the problems with the Sports Professional's advice.

FITNESS TALK

Do you have a question about exercise? Write to Steven, the Sports Professional, for help and good advice.

1. John: I never exercise. I drive to work, and I sit all day. I hate sports, and I don't like the gym. I know it's a good idea to exercise, but how do I start? _____

2. Amy: I'm really busy this year. I'm going to school, and I'm working part-time at night. I like exercise, but I don't have a lot of time. Help! _____

3. Bill: I do weight training at the gym every day. I usually love exercise, but these days, it's boring. I think I need a break. What do you think?

a. The Sports Professional: Slowly add exercise to your weekly routine. Walk or ride a bike to work – don't drive. Use the stairs, not the elevator. Clean the house, or do the laundry. Just do something – and start today!

b. The Sports Professional: You're right. You need a break. Try exergaming for a change. There are a lot of different types of activities, and each one helps your body in a different way. Don't stop your weight training, and remember, running is always good for you, too.

c. The Sports Professional: Yes, I know the problem, but try and make time. Experts say we need 30 minutes of exercise five times a week. So, do aerobics for 15 minutes in the morning. Go to school. Then go running for 15 minutes in the evening after work.

C Read the advice column again. Then answer the questions.

1. Is John getting enough exercise these days? _____
2. Does John like sports? _____
3. Amy is busy this year. What is she doing? _____
4. What is Amy's problem? _____
5. How often does Bill go to the gym? _____
6. What does Bill do at the gym? _____

2 Write your own advice.

A Look again at the advice column on page 56. Find two imperatives the Sports Professional uses in each piece of advice.

Try exergaming for a change.

B Make imperatives for advice. Match the verbs with the words and expressions.

(Don't)	be	aerobics in the morning	*Don't be shy.*
	buy	at least five times a week	*Buy some good running shoes.*
	do	shy	
	drive	some good running shoes	
	exercise	to work	
	watch	TV all the time	

C Read the problems. Reply to each person. Give two pieces of advice using imperatives. Use the ideas above or your own ideas.

1. **Joe:** I watch sports on TV all the time. I'm watching the Olympics this month. It's great, but I don't do any sports. What sports are fun?
The Sports Professional: *Try a lot of different sports. I like volleyball, tennis, and swimming. Also,* ___

2. **Anita:** This fall, we're playing soccer at school. I'm not enjoying it very much, especially when it's cold! Also, I'm not very good. Help!
The Sports Professional: ___

3. **David:** I like exercise, but I'm lazy! I usually exercise for two or three weeks, but then I need a break. Do you have any advice?
The Sports Professional: ___

Unit 7 Progress chart

What can you do? Mark the boxes. ☑ = I can . . . ? = I need to review how to . . .	To review, go back to these pages in the Student's Book.
Grammar — make present continuous statements.	66 and 67
ask present continuous questions.	68 and 69
Vocabulary — name at least 6 words to talk about the weather.	65, 66, and 67
name at least 10 sports and kinds of exercise.	67 and 68
Conversation strategies — ask follow-up questions to keep the conversation going.	70 and 71
react to things people say with *That's . . .* expressions.	71
Writing — use imperatives to give instructions and advice.	73

Shopping

Lesson A / Clothes

1 Do a crossword puzzle.

Vocabulary **A** Complete the crossword puzzle. Write the names of the clothes.

Down

1.

3.

5.

7.

8.

10.

11.

Crossword puzzle:

2. h i g h h e e l s

Across

2.

4.

6.

9.

11.

12.

B Now find the five highlighted letters in the puzzle. What do they spell?

____ ____ ____ ____ _s_

58

2 I want to spend some money!

Grammar | Complete the conversations with the correct form of the verbs.

1. Mia   Let's go shopping. I _need to buy_ (need / buy) some new clothes.
   Rick OK. Where do you _____ (want / go) ?
   Mia   To the mall. I _____ (need / get)
         some new jeans. And I _____ (have / get)
         a couple of new suits for work.
   Rick Listen. You go. I think I _____ (want / stay)
         home. I _____ (not need / buy) anything,
         and I _____ (want / check) my email.
   Mia   OK!

2. Will I have a date with Megan tonight. She _____ (want / go)
         to an expensive restaurant.
   Ana   Really? Do you have any good clothes?
         Those old jeans are terrible. And you know Megan –
         she _____ (like / wear) designer clothes.
   Will I know, but I _____ (like / wear) my jeans!
         And I _____ (not want / go) to a
         restaurant anyway. I _____ (want / go) to a movie.
   Ana   Oh, there's the phone. Hello? . . . Will, it's Megan. She's sick.
   Will Oh, no! Well, now I _____ (not have / change) my clothes!

3 About you

Grammar and vocabulary | Unscramble the questions. Then write true answers.

1. A to the movies / do / like / What / to / wear / you ? _What do you like to wear to the movies?_
   B _____

2. A nice / have / When / do / to / clothes / you / wear ? _____
   B _____

3. A you / Do / a / have / uniform / to / wear ? _____
   B _____

4. A buy / Do / like / you / to / online / things ? _____
   B _____

5. A clothes / do / What / want / you / buy / to ? _____
   B _____

6. A do / go / like / Where / you / to / shopping ? _____
   B _____

Lesson B / Things to buy

1 Accessories

Vocabulary | Write the words under the pictures using *a* or *some*.

1. _some jeans_

2. _a dress_

3. _____

4. _____

5. _____

6. _____

7. _____

8. _____

9. _____

10. _____

11. _____

12. _____

13. _____

14. _____

15. _____

16. _____

2 Colors

Vocabulary | Complete the color words in the box. Then answer the questions, and complete the chart. Write three colors to answer each question, if possible.

r _e_ d   y_____ w   b_____ k   p_____ e   w_____ e
o_____ e   b_____ e   g_____ n   b_____ n   g_____ y

What colors . . .			
do you like to wear?	blue		
are you wearing right now?			
do you never wear?			
are in your home?			
are your favorites?			
are popular right now?			
are in your country's flag?			

3 How much is this?

Grammar | **A** Complete the conversations. Use *this, that, these,* or *those.*

1. Lena   Um, excuse me. How much is ___*that*___ dress?

    Clerk   The red dress? It's $325.

    Lena   Oh. And how about _____ shoes?

    Clerk   They're $149.

    Lena   Oh, really. And what about _____ T-shirts?
    Are they expensive, too?

    Clerk   They're $49.

    Lena   Oh, well. Thanks anyway.

2. Tito   Excuse me.

    Seller   Yes?

    Tito   How much are _____ umbrellas?

    Seller   They're $19.99.

    Tito $19.99? Really?

    Seller   Oh, wait. Sorry. _____ umbrella is $4.99.
    _____ umbrellas over here are $19.99.

    Tito   OK, so I want _____ umbrella, please.

B Look at the pictures. Write questions and answers.

1.
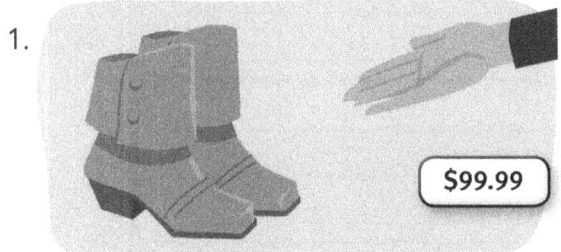

$99.99

A   *How much are those boots?*
B   _____

2.

$38

A   _____
B   _____

3.

$40

A   _____
B   _____

4.
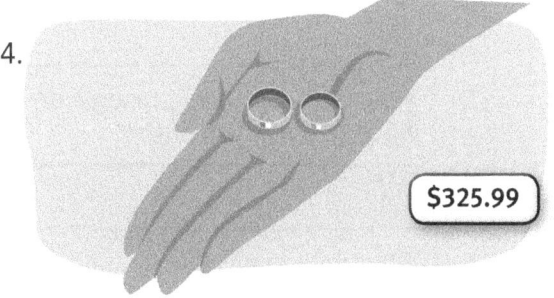

$325.99

A   _____
B   _____

/ # Can I help you?

1 Um, uh, oh!

Complete the chart with the "conversation sounds" and expressions in the box.

✓I know.	Let's see.	Really?	Uh,	Um,	Yeah.
Let me think.	Oh.	Right.	Uh-huh.	Well,	

You want to show you agree.	You are surprised.	You need time to think.
I know.		

2 About you

Answer the questions with true information. Start each answer with a "time to think" expression.

1. What's your favorite color?

   Let me think. . . . I guess it's green. _____

2. What's your favorite thing to wear?

   _____

3. How often do you shop online?

   _____

4. How much do jeans cost these days?

   _____

5. How many birthday presents do you have to buy this month?

   _____

6. Does your family like to shop for clothes together?

   _____

③ Are you listening?

Conversation strategies | **Complete the conversation with the correct expressions.**

Roberto	Mom, I have to get some things for college.
Mother	<u> _Uh-huh._ </u> What do you need to get? (Uh-huh. / Let me think.)
Roberto	_____ . . . I need to get a new computer and . . . (Um, let's see. / Really!)
Mother	_____ They're expensive. (Let me think. / Oh, really?)
Roberto	I know. But I have to go online a lot for my classes.
Mother	Well, OK. And what else do you want?
Roberto	_____ I want to get a new cell phone and . . . (Uh-huh. / Uh, well . . .)
Mother	_____ I'm surprised. I mean, (Oh, / Um,) you usually don't call, so . . .
Roberto	Well, I text sometimes. Anyway, _____ Oh, yes, and (let's see. / uh-huh.) I have to get some new sneakers.
Mother	_____ You really need new sneakers. Those sneakers are really old. (Let me think. / Uh-huh.)
Roberto	And what else? _____ What else do I need to get? (Oh, really? / Uh, let's see.)
Mother	Well, there's one more thing you need to get . . .
Roberto	What's that?
Mother	A job! You need to pay for these things!

1 Online shopping

Reading | **A** Read the article. Who likes to shop online? Who doesn't like to shop online? Check (✓) the correct boxes.

	Likes to shop online	Doesn't like to shop online
Sarah	☐	☐
Matt	☐	☐
Kevin	☐	☐
Susana	☐	☐

Do you like to shop online?

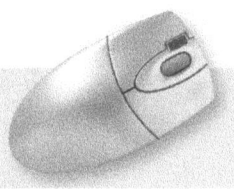

These days *everything* is for sale online – from movie tickets and food, to cars and houses. More and more people download music, movies, magazines, and books. It's easy and convenient. But not *everyone* likes to shop online.

Sarah Cho

"I never shop on the Internet because I like to pay cash. I don't have a credit card, and I don't want to get one. Also, I don't like to spend a lot of time online. I guess I'm not a big fan of shopping."

Matt Carson

"I work long hours – from 9:00 in the morning to 9:00 or 10:00 at night. A lot of stores close at 9:00. But the Internet never closes. I mean, I often shop at 1:00 in the morning. And the prices online are usually really cheap."

Kevin Parker

"There isn't a shopping center near my house. I have to drive an hour to the mall. Online shopping is very convenient. I buy movies, books, clothes, and food online. I never need to go out to a store."

Susana Rivera

"I like to shop with friends. We get up early and go to the mall together. We have a great time. We have lunch and look at the clothes together. When you shop online, you don't spend time with friends. You're alone."

B Read the article again. Then write *Sarah*, *Matt*, *Kevin*, or *Susana* next to the statements.

1. "I don't like to shop online or in stores!" _____*Sarah*_____

2. "I like to shop online because I never have to leave my home." _____

3. "I like to shop online because the prices aren't expensive." _____

4. "I don't like to shop online because I like to go to the mall with friends." _____

5. "I like to shop online because I don't have time during the day." _____

6. "I don't like to shop online because I don't like to go on the Internet." _____

2 What do you think?

A Why do people like to shop online? Why do people hate to shop online? Check (✓) the correct box.

I like to shop online . . .	I hate to shop online . . .	Reasons
☐	☐	because I always buy things I don't need.
☐	☐	because it's easy to compare prices.
☐	☐	because it's convenient.
☐	☐	because you don't always have to pay sales tax.
☐	☐	because I often get "spam" emails from shopping websites.

B Answer these questions. Try to write more than *Yes* or *No*.

1. Do you live near a mall or shopping center? _____

2. Do you have time to shop during the week? _____

3. Do you like to go online? _____

4. Do you use a credit card? _____

C Write a short paragraph. Use your ideas from part B, and give reasons. Start like this:
I like to shop online because . . . **or** *I don't like to shop online because . . .*

_____

_____

_____

_____

Unit 8 Progress chart

What can you do? Mark the boxes. ✓ = I can . . . ? = I need to review how to . . .	To review, go back to these pages in the Student's Book.
Grammar	
☐ use *like to*, *want to*, *need to*, and *have to* with other verbs.	76 and 77
☐ ask questions with *How much . . . ?*	78 and 79
☐ use *this*, *these*, *that*, and *those*.	79
Vocabulary	
☐ name at least 12 kinds of clothes.	75, 76, and 77
☐ name at least 12 accessories.	78 and 79
☐ name at least 8 color words.	78
Conversation strategies	
☐ use "time to think" expressions like *Um, . . .* and *Let's see . . . .*	80
☐ use *Uh-huh* and *Oh*, to show that I agree or I'm surprised.	81
Writing	
☐ use *because* to give reasons.	83

A wide world

Lesson A / Sightseeing

 Take a tour!

Vocabulary **A** Complete these suggestions for tourists.

1. In South Korea, visit
   an island .

2. In New York, take pictures
   from a _____ .

3. In Germany, visit an old
   _____ .

4. See a _____ of a
   famous writer in Paris.

5. In Rio de Janeiro, spend a
   day at the _____ .

6. In Egypt, walk around the
   _____ .

7. In London, see a famous
   _____ .

8. Go up a _____ and
   get a good view of Tokyo.

9. Take a _____ of the
   city in Sydney.

Grammar and vocabulary **B** Can you do any of the things in part A in your city or town? Write true sentences.

1. _In my area, you can visit an island._ **or** _In my area, you can't visit an island._
2. _____
3. _____
4. _____
5. _____
6. _____
7. _____
8. _____
9. _____

2 What can you do in Toronto?

Grammar **A** Read the guidebook. What can you do in Toronto? Complete the chart below.

TORONTO, CANADA

1. The CN Tower
Get a good view of the city from 553 meters (1,814 feet). A restaurant, shops, and a glass floor!
Hours: 10:00 a.m. to 11:00 p.m.

2. Casa Loma
Toronto's only castle. Call for a tour.
Open 9:30 a.m. to 5:00 p.m. (Last entry at 4:00 p.m.)

3. Yorkville
Walk around a lively historic neighborhood! Outdoor cafés, shops, and movie theaters.

4. The Art Gallery of Ontario
Hours: 10:00 a.m. to 5:30 p.m.

5. Centre Island
Take the ferry to Centre Island. Enjoy beautiful parks, great restaurants, and a children's amusement park.
Open all day.

6. Harbourfront Centre
Right on Lake Ontario, this huge center has everything for all the family. Ice skating, art, cafés, a music garden, shops, sailing, and boat tours. In the summer, there are outdoor concerts, a market, and special events.
Open from 10:00 a.m. to 9:00 p.m.

On a rainy day	On a sunny day	In the evening	With children
You can go to the Art Gallery of Ontario.			

B Complete the conversations with *can* or *can't*.

1. Jill What ___can___ you do at Harbourfront Centre?

    Dan Let's see . . . you _____ rent a boat. And at night, you _____ go to an outdoor concert.

    Jill Sounds great! _____ we go right now?

    Dan No, we _____ . It opens at 10:00 a.m., and it's only 7:30 a.m. now. It's really early.

    Jill Oh, you're right. Well, _____ we go to a café for breakfast?

    Dan Yes, we _____ do that. Let's go!

2. Yoshi I'm tired today. I don't want to go on another walking tour! Where _____ we go to relax?

    Keiko Let's go to Yorkville. We _____ have a nice lunch and see a movie.

    Yoshi OK, but we _____ spend a lot of money. We need to save our money for shopping!

1 What countries do you know?

Vocabulary | **A** Complete the names of the countries. Then write the countries in the chart below.

1. S _p_ ai _n_
2. ____ ____ str ____ l ____ ____
3. ____ or ____ cc ____
4. C ____ st ____ ____ ic ____
5. R ____ ss ____ ____
6. M ____ x ____ c ____

7. P ____ r ____
8. Fr ____ nc ____
9. S ____ ____ th
   K ____ r ____ ____
10. Ch ____ n ____
11. Th ____ ____ l ____ nd

12. I ____ d ____ ____
13. J ____ p ____ n
14. C ____ n ____ d ____
15. Br ____ z ____ l

I know a lot about . . .			
I don't know a lot about . . .			
They speak English in . . .			
I love the food from . . .			
I don't want to go to . . .			

B Look at the pictures. What kinds of food are these dishes? Write the nationalities.

1. _____ _Japanese_ _____

2. _____

3. _____

4. _____

C Complete the chart.

Food I like	Food I don't like	Food I want to try	Food I can cook
Korean			_French_

2 Where in the world?

Vocabulary | **Complete the crossword puzzle.**

1.											
2. A	N	3. T	A	R	C	T	4. I	C	A	5.
		T					I			A
		6.						C		
		U					T			A
7.			R		8.		A			
		K				L			A
	9.	E					Y			A
		Y			10.					

Across

2. There are no cities in this cold, icy region.
6. This country is in both Europe and Asia.
7. This large region includes Japan and South Korea.
9. Beijing, Shanghai, and Hong Kong are in this country.
10. This long, thin country is in South America.

Down

1. They speak both French and English in this North American country.
3. They speak this language in Turkey.
4. Rome, Venice, and Milan are cities in this European country.
5. This large country is in Oceania.
8. They speak this language in Thailand.

3 About you

Grammar | **Unscramble the questions. Then write true answers.**

1. can / sports / play / What / your best friend ?
   A _What sports can your best friend play?_
   B _____

2. food / mother / make / Can / Mexican / your ?
   A _____
   B _____

3. speak / you / languages / can / What ?
   A _____
   B _____

4. your / speak / English / parents / Can ?
   A _____
   B _____

1 What's this? What are these?

Conversation strategies What are the things in the pictures? Write sentences. Use the words in the box.

| candy | dress | drink | ✓ musical instrument | sandwich | shoe |

1. *It's a kind of musical instrument.*
   It's called an erhu.

2. *They're a kind of*
   They're called
   _____

3. _____
   _____
   _____

4. _____
   _____
   _____

5. _____
   _____
   _____

6. _____
   _____
   _____

2 What's an *Inukshuk*?

Conversation strategies

Complete the sentences. Then unscramble the letters from the boxes to find the answer to the question.

1. A sneaker is a kind of [s] _h_ _o_ _e_ .
2. A *tortilla* is kind of like a _p_ ___ ___ ___ [a] ___ ___ .
3. A *balalaika* is like a _g_ ___ ___ [t] ___ ___ .
4. *Gazpacho* is a kind of tomato _s_ ___ [ ] _p_ .
5. *Lassi* is kind of like a ___ ___ ___ _k_ _s_ ___ ___ ___ [e] .
6. Volleyball is a kind of ___ _p_ ___ _r_ [ ] .

What's an *Inukshuk*?

It's like a _s_ ___ ___ _t_ ___ _e_ . You can see them in Alaska and Greenland.

3 It's a kind of pot.

Conversation strategies

Complete the conversations. Use *like*, *kind of like*, or *a kind of*.

1. A That's a beautiful dish!
   B Thanks. Actually, it's _a kind of_ pot. It's Japanese.
   A Can you cook with it? It looks so pretty.
   B Yeah! You can make Japanese food _____
      yosenabe in it.
   A Like what?
   B Yosenabe. It's _____ soup.

2. A What can you buy at the market?
   B Well, you can buy food from different countries, things
      _____ fruit. You can buy durians . . .
   A What's a durian?
   B It's _____ fruit.
   A Really?
   B Yeah. It's _____ a melon.
   A Is it good?
   B Yes, I love it.

1 FAQs about Paris

Reading **A** Read the website. Write the correct question heading for each paragraph.

> Where can you eat in Paris?   ✓ What are great places to visit in Paris?
> What do people wear in Paris?   How can I travel around Paris?

http://www.parispage...   🔍

THE PARIS PAGE

Find out all you need to know about Paris! You can send your questions here for other travelers to answer. Or share your information about your trip to Paris.

Frequently Asked Questions (FAQs)

What are great places to visit in Paris?

You have to see the Eiffel Tower on your first visit. Then go to the Louvre. It's a very large and famous art museum. There are also beautiful gardens near it. After that, you can visit the Latin Quarter. It's a very old neighborhood. It has a lot of historic buildings, museums, and great shopping. More

It's easy to travel in Paris. There are trains, buses, and subways. Try the subway system, called the Metro. There are 301 Metro stations in the city. Every building in Paris is near a Metro station, so it's very convenient, too! More

Parisians love food. There are amazing cafés, bistros, and other kinds of restaurants everywhere in the city. You can relax at an outdoor café all day. Cafés open early in the morning and usually close late in the evening. More

Parisians like to "dress up" and wear designer clothes. They don't usually wear shorts, sneakers, or T-shirts to restaurants or concerts. You can wear casual clothes and shoes in Paris, but try to look nice. More

Next

B Read the website again. Then write *T* (true) or *F* (false) for each sentence. Correct the false sentences.

1. The Louvre is a famous garden in Paris. *F* *The Louvre is a famous art museum in Paris.*
2. The Latin Quarter is a historic building. _____
3. The Metro is a museum in Paris. _____
4. A bistro is a kind of restaurant. _____
5. Cafés open late in Paris. _____
6. Parisians like to wear casual clothes when they go out. _____

72

2 FAQs about your country

Writing | **A** Complete each sentence with three things about your city or country.
Make lists and use commas.

1. _El Salvador_ is famous for _its beautiful beaches, outdoor markets, and great food_ .
2. _____ is famous for _____ .
3. There are great places to see. You can visit _____ .
4. The people usually wear _____ .

B Imagine you are looking at a travel website about your country or city.
Write answers to these questions.

```
○○○                              TRAVEL
  1.  I often travel there on business, but I don't usually have a lot of time. Where can I go and
      what can I see in one day?
      _____
      _____
      _____

  2.  I want to visit this summer, but I don't have a lot of money. What can I do for free?
      _____
      _____
      _____

  3.  Where can I meet local people? What traditional things can I see or do?
      _____
      _____
```

Unit 9 Progress chart

What can you do? Mark the boxes. ☑ = I can . . . ? = I need to review how to . . .	To review, go back to these pages in the Student's Book.
Grammar ☐ use *can* and *can't* to talk about things to do in a city.	86 and 87
☐ use *can* and *can't* to talk about ability.	88 and 89
Vocabulary ☐ use at least 10 new sightseeing words.	86 and 87
☐ name at least 15 countries and 5 regions.	88
☐ name at least 10 nationalities and 10 languages.	88 and 89
Conversation strategies ☐ use *a kind of* and *kind of like* to explain new words.	90
☐ use *like* to give examples.	91
Writing ☐ use commas to separate items in a list.	93

Busy lives

Lesson A / A night at home

 What did they do last night?

Grammar | What did these people do last night? What didn't they do? Complete two sentences for each picture. Use the simple past.

stay home / visit her parents

1. Kate _stayed home_____ .
   She _didn't visit her parents_____ .

watch TV / practice her guitar

2. Rita _____ .
   She _____ .

study English / cook dinner

3. Mee-Sun _____ .
   She _____ .

play chess / watch a movie

4. Ali and Sam _____ .
   They _____ .

listen to music / email friends

5. Emil _____ .
   He _____ .

invite friends over / clean the house

6. Joe and Ken _____ .
   They _____ .

2 How was your weekend?

Grammar | **Complete Grace's email. Use the simple past.**

> **New Message**
>
> To: Paulina Lopez
> From: Grace Chen
> Subject: How was your weekend?
>
> Hi Paulina!
>
> I really *enjoyed* (enjoy) the weekend! I _____ (invite) a friend
> over on Saturday. She's my co-worker, and she's very nice. We
> _____ (play) tennis in the morning and _____ (stay) at the
> tennis club for lunch. Then we _____ (practice) yoga and
> _____ (walk) in the park.
>
> In the evening, we _____ (watch) a movie and _____ (cook)
> a big dinner. We _____ (talk) a lot, but we _____ (not talk)
> about work. And we _____ (not watch) TV all day – a nice change!
>
> Then on Sunday, I _____ (study) English and _____ (clean) the
> house. Hey! You _____ (not call) me on Sunday! Call me soon, OK?
> Tell me about your weekend.
>
> Grace

3 About you

Grammar and vocabulary | **Write true sentences about your weekend. Use the simple past. Add more information.**

1. invite a friend over   *I invited a friend over for dinner.* **or** *I didn't invite a friend over for dinner.*

2. stay home   _____

3. study for an exam   _____

4. clean the house   _____

5. call a friend   _____

6. check my email   _____

7. chat online   _____

8. practice my English   _____

9. listen to music   _____

10. rent a car   _____

11. cook a big meal   _____

12. exercise   _____

A weekly planner

Read Jenna's planner. Then complete the sentences below. Use the simple past of the verbs in the box.

SUNDAY

Movie with Meg 1:00 ✓

Romeo and Juliet –
Grand Theater 2:00 ✗

Homework ✗

MONDAY

Read The Pearl ✓

Read art magazine ✗

Homework ✓

TUESDAY

Write book report on
The Pearl ✓

Write history paper ✗

Homework ✓

WEDNESDAY

Piano lesson 4:30 ✗

Doctor's appointment
2:00 ✓

Homework ✓

THURSDAY

Call: Mom ✓
   Felipe ✓
   Lia ✓

Make dinner 6:30 ✗

Homework ✓

FRIDAY

Alison's party 7:30 ✓

Mike 8:00 ✗

Homework ✓

SATURDAY

Shopping! Need new:
   shoes ✗
   jacket ✓

Homework ✗

---

buy	do	go	have	make	read	✓see	write

1. On Sunday, Jenna _____*saw*_____ a movie.
   She _*didn't see*_ a play.

2. On Monday, Jenna _____ a book in English.
   She _____ a magazine.

3. Jenna _____ a book report on Tuesday.
   She _____ a history paper.

4. Jenna _____ a doctor's appointment on Wednesday.
   She _____ a piano lesson this week.

5. On Thursday, Jenna _____ a lot of phone calls.
   She _____ dinner.

6. On Friday, Jenna _____ to a party.
   She _____ out with Mike.

7. Jenna _____ a new jacket on Saturday.
   She _____ new shoes.

8. Jenna _____ homework every school day.
   She _____ homework on the weekend.

2 About you

Grammar and vocabulary **A** Complete the questions in the questionnaire. Use the simple past of the verbs in the box. Then write true answers. Write more than *yes* or *no*.

do	eat	✓go	have	make	see	speak	take	write

QUESTIONNAIRE: Did you . . . ?

1. __Did__ you __go__ out a lot last week?
   Yes, I did. I went out every night last week. **or** _No, I didn't. I stayed home._ _____

2. _____ you and your family _____ dinner in front of the TV last night?
   _____

3. _____ you _____ anything interesting last weekend?
   _____

4. _____ you _____ in a restaurant on Friday night?
   _____

5. _____ your class _____ a test or an exam last week?
   _____

6. _____ you _____ dinner every night last week?
   _____

7. _____ your best friend _____ you an email yesterday?
   _____

8. _____ your parents _____ a movie on Saturday night?
   _____

9. _____ you _____ to a lot of friends in class yesterday?
   _____

B Write a sentence about each day last week. Write one thing you did each day.

1. Monday _____ _____

2. Tuesday _____

3. Wednesday _____

4. Thursday _____

5. Friday _____

6. Saturday _____

7. Sunday _____

1 Responding to news

Conversation strategies **A** **Complete the conversations. Circle and write the best response.**

1. A   I bought a new TV today.

   B   _Good for you!_

   (a.) Good for you!

   b. I'm sorry to hear that.

   c. Good luck!

2. A   I'm 25 today!

   B   _____

   a. I'm sorry to hear that.

   b. Good luck!

   c. Happy birthday!

3. A   My wife had a baby girl last night.

   B   _____

   a. Good for you!

   b. Happy birthday!

   c. Congratulations!

4. A   I have a job interview today.

   B   _____

   a. I'm sorry to hear that.

   b. Good luck!

   c. Happy birthday!

5. A   I finally passed my English exam.

   B   _____

   a. Thank goodness!

   b. I'm sorry to hear that.

   c. Good luck!

6. A   I didn't get the job I wanted.

   B   _____

   a. I'm sorry to hear that.

   b. Thank goodness!

   c. Good for you!

B **Your friend tells you some news, and you respond. Write the conversations.**

1. Your friend bought a new car, and he got a bargain.

   > _I bought a new car today. I got a bargain._   _Good for you!_

2. Your friend got 100% on her English exam.

3. Your friend finally got a job.

4. Your friend wanted to go on vacation, but he has no money.

2 You did?

A Complete the conversations with the expressions in the box.

✓You did?   You did?   You did?   Good luck!   I'm sorry to hear that.   Good for you.

1. Lilly   Did you have a busy day?

   Beth   Yeah, I'm exhausted. I went shopping downtown.

   Lilly   _____You_____ _____did?_____ Did you buy anything?

   Beth   Yes, I bought a new suit. And a blouse and shoes.

   Lilly   _____ _____ _____

   Beth   And then I had lunch with Maria, and we talked all afternoon. How about you?

   Lilly   I cleaned the house, did the laundry, and made dinner.

   Beth   _____ _____ That's great! I'm starving! Let's eat!

2. Jun   Did you have a good week?

   José   Actually, no. I had five exams.

   Jun   _____ _____ That's awful. Did you pass?

   José   Well, I passed three and failed two.

   Jun   Oh. _____ _____ _____ _____ _____

   José   And I have two exams tomorrow, too.

   Jun   _____ _____ Study hard!

B Write two responses for each piece of news.

1. I had a terrible vacation in Hawaii.

   You did? _I'm sorry to hear that._

2. I took my driver's test yesterday.

   _____ _____

3. I wrote an article for a magazine last month.

   _____ _____

4. My friend and I worked all weekend.

   _____ _____

1 A busy birthday . . .

Reading **A** Look at the four pictures. Then read Peter's blog. Number the pictures in order from 1 to 4.

☐   1   ☐   ☐

Friday, May 28 11:45 p.m.

I had a crazy day today. I had an English exam, and it's my birthday!

I had the exam at 8:30 this morning. I needed to study, so I woke up early – at 6:30 a.m. I took a shower, made some coffee, and studied for about an hour. Well, the coffee didn't work. I fell asleep! I woke up at 8:20 with my head on my books. I had ten minutes before the test started!

I ran outside, got on my bike, and went to English class. I got there right at 8:30, but guess what! The teacher never came! My classmates and I waited about half an hour. Then we left. It's great. Now I can really study for the exam.

I had breakfast, and then I went to my next class – math. ☹ I think math is really hard, but I have to take it. My teacher talked for an hour. I wanted to write some notes, but I fell asleep. I need to borrow my friend's notes.

After I finished class, I met my friend Louisa, and we went to a movie together. It was my birthday, so she paid! Great! We saw a new romantic drama. You know, I usually like drama movies a lot, but I didn't like that movie very much.

When I got home from the movie, my mother called and sang "Happy Birthday" to me. Now I have to stay up and finish a paper for a class tomorrow. I hope I don't fall asleep again!

Posted by Peter Miller

0 comments

B Read the blog again. Then answer the questions. Give reasons for the answers.

1. Did Peter get up late? _No, he didn't. He needed to study._

2. Did Peter take an English exam? _____

3. Did he listen to his math teacher? _____

4. Did he go out with a friend? _____

5. Did Peter's mother call? _____

6. Do you think he's a good student? _____

2 My last birthday

Writing | **A Read the blog on page 80 again. Match the two parts of each sentence.**

1. Peter studied when ___c___
2. Peter had breakfast after _____
3. When Peter went to his math class, _____
4. Peter finished classes. Then _____
5. Peter saw a movie before _____

a. he went home.
b. he fell asleep again.
✓c. he got up in the morning.
d. he met his friend Louisa.
e. he left his English class.

B Think about a day you remember well. Answer these questions. Write more than *yes* or *no*.

1. Did you work or have classes? _____
2. Did you go out with friends? _____
3. Did you do something fun? _____
4. Did you eat any of your favorite foods? _____
5. Did you go to any stores? _____
6. Did you get home late? _____

**C Write a paragraph for your own blog. Use your ideas from part B.
Use *before*, *after*, *when*, or *then*, if possible.**

I remember my last birthday. I _____

_____

_____

_____

_____

Unit 10 Progress chart

What can you do? Mark the boxes. ✓ = I can . . . ? = I need to review how to . . .	To review, go back to these pages in the Student's Book.
Grammar	
☐ make simple past statements with regular verbs.	98 and 99
☐ make simple past statements with irregular verbs.	100 and 101
☐ ask simple past *yes-no* questions.	101
Vocabulary	
☐ make simple past forms of at least 12 regular verbs.	98 and 99
☐ make simple past forms of at least 8 irregular verbs.	100 and 101
☐ use time expressions with the simple past.	101
Conversation strategies	
☐ use responses like *Good for you!* and *Congratulations!*	102 and 103
☐ use *You did?* to show I'm listening, surprised, or interested.	103
Writing	
☐ use *before*, *after*, *when*, and *then* to order events.	105

1 Yesterday

Vocabulary | Complete the sentences. Use the words in the box.

| busy | ✓happy | nervous | nice | quiet | scared |

1. Yesterday was my birthday. My friends had a party for me, and I got a lot of presents. I was very __happy__ .
2. My family and I live in a very small town. There are no clubs or movie theaters. My town is really _____ – especially at night.
3. I started a new job yesterday. I was really _____ of my new boss.
4. I had a lot of things to do yesterday. I was pretty _____ .
5. My best friend's parents are friendly. They're very _____ .
6. We had a French test last week. I was really _____ , but I passed.

2 It was fun!

Vocabulary | Choose the best two words to complete each sentence. Cross out the wrong word.

I remember my first driving lesson. Before I met the teacher, I was really ~~scary~~ / **nervous** / **scared**. But then I relaxed because he was very **nice** / **strict** / **friendly**. The lesson was **awful** / **good** / **fun** because I didn't make a lot of mistakes. I was pretty good. At the end of the lesson, I was **exhausted** / **lazy** / **tired**. It was hard work! After ten lessons, I took my test, but I didn't pass. I wasn't **awful** / **pleased** / **happy**. But I passed three weeks later. Now I can drive my dad's **nice** / **new** / **awful** car.

3 I remember . . .

| **Complete the conversations with *was, wasn't, were,* or *weren't*.**

1. Sally   Do you remember your first date, Grandpa?

    Grandpa   Yes. I ___*was*___ 16, and the girl _____ in my class.

    We _____ classmates. We went to the movies.

    Sally   _____ you nervous?

    Grandpa   No, I _____ . It _____ a lot of fun.

    Sally   Do you remember her name?

    Grandpa   Yes. Grandma!

2. Paula   I remember my first day of high school.

    It _____ a hot day, and I went with

    two of my friends.

    Kenton   _____ you scared?

    Paula   No, we _____ really scared, but I

    guess we _____ a little nervous.

    Kenton   _____ the teachers friendly?

    Paula   Yes, they _____ very nice.

    Thank goodness.

3. Sun-Hee   Do you remember your first college English class?

    Carla   Yes, it _____ last year. I _____ very good at

    English, and I made a lot of mistakes. My partner's

    English _____ very good, so he _____

    very happy with me!

    Sun-Hee   _____ he smart? I mean, intelligent?

    Carla   Yes, he _____ .

    Sun-Hee   So, was your first class fun?

    Carla   No, it _____ . In fact,

    it _____ awful.

Lesson B / Vacations

1 About you

Grammar and vocabulary **A** Unscramble the questions. Then write true answers.

1. trip or vacation / was / last / your / When ?

   A _When was your last trip or vacation?_

   B _____

2. go / did / Where / exactly / you ?

   A _____

   B _____

3. weather / like / was / the / What ?

   A _____

   B _____

4. you / there / do / did / What ?

   A _____

   B _____

5. were / there / How / you / long ?

   A _____

   B _____

Grammar **B** Read about Emi's first trip to the park with a friend. Write questions for the answers.

"We weren't very old – I think I was eight, and my friend was ten. We went to the park, but my mother didn't know. We had a great time! We went swimming in the pool. I remember it was a beautiful day – warm and sunny. We were there about an hour. Then we got hungry, so we went home. When we got back, my mother wasn't too happy."

1. A _How old was Emi?_

   B Eight.

2. A _____

   B To the park.

3. A _____

   B Her friend.

4. A _____

   B They went swimming.

5. A _____

   B Warm and sunny.

6. A _____

   B About an hour.

84

2 *Get* and *go*

Vocabulary   **A** Which of these expressions do you use with *get*? Which do you use with *go*? Which can you use with *get* and *go*? Complete the chart.

✓back	to bed	scared	swimming	to the movies	a view of something
✓lost	a gift	skiing	(an) autograph	snorkeling	along with someone
home	hiking	camping	on vacation	a bad sunburn	to see a concert / movie
sick	biking	married	up early or late	on a road trip	to the beach

get	*go*	*get* and *go*
lost		back

B Complete the questions with *get* or *go*. Then write your own answers.

1. A What time do you ___go **or** get___ to bed on weeknights?

    B _____

2. A How often do you _____ swimming?

    B _____

3. A Did you _____ a bad sunburn last year?

    B _____

4. A What did you _____ for your last birthday?

    B _____

5. A Can you think of someone you don't _____ along with?

    B _____

6. A Where do you want to _____ on vacation this year?

    B _____

7. A Do you _____ up early in the morning?

    B _____

1 Asking questions

Conversation strategies | **Complete each conversation with two questions.**

1. Sadie   How was your weekend?

   Bill   It was awful. We went hang gliding. I hated it!

   Sadie   That's too bad.

   Bill   Yeah. Anyway, how about you?

   What did you do?

   Did you do anything special?

   Sadie   Well, we rented a car and went camping.

   Bill   That sounds nice.

2. Dirk   Did you go out last night?

   Leo   Yeah, I met a friend and went to a club.

   _____

   _____

   Dirk   Oh, I went to the laundromat and did my
   laundry. I didn't do anything exciting.

3. Shira   I went to the concert last Saturday.

   Jaz   I did, too! The band sounded great.

   _____

   _____

   Shira   Oh, it was fantastic. Well, anyway, it's 11:30.

   Jaz   Yeah, it's late. See you tomorrow.

4. Gabor   So, did you work last weekend?

   Koji   Yeah, Saturday and Sunday. We were really busy.

   _____

   _____

   Gabor   Let's see . . . I went shopping, um, and saw
   a movie. Then on Sunday, I played tennis,
   made dinner, . . .

   Koji   I guess you were busy, too!

2 Well, anyway, . . .

A Use *anyway* three times in this conversation. Leave two of the blanks empty.

Mirka   Where were you last week? Were you away?

Arlen   Yes, I was in Mexico on business.

Mirka   Mexico? What was that like?

Arlen   Oh, great. The customers there are really nice.
_____ I always enjoy my trips to Mexico.
The people are so friendly.

Mirka   That's nice. _____ So you're traveling a
lot these days.

Arlen   Yeah. About six times a year. _____ ,
what about you? Did you have a good week?

Mirka   Not bad. I had a lot of meetings – you know, the
usual. _____ , do you want to go out
tonight? We can have dinner maybe.

Arlen   Sure. We can meet after work.

Mirka   OK. Well, _____ , I have to go. See you later.

B Use the instructions to complete the conversations.

1. Friend   What do you usually do on the weekends?

   You   *I usually go out with friends. What about you?*
   (Answer. Then ask a question about your friend.)

   Friend   Me? I usually go to see a movie. Sometimes a friend and I go camping or hiking.

2. Friend   I'm enjoying my new job. My boss is OK, and the people are nice. We get
   along – it's a friendly place.

   You   That's nice. _____
   (Change the topic. Invite your friend for dinner tomorrow.)

   Friend   Tomorrow? Sounds great. What time? Seven?

3. Friend   What did you do for your last birthday?

   You   _____
   (Answer. Then end the conversation. It's late.)

   Friend   OK. Talk to you later.

4. Friend   So how was your weekend?

   You   _____
   (Answer. Then change the topic. Invite your friend to do something fun next weekend.)

   Friend   Sure. Sounds like fun.

1 My first job

Reading | **A** Read the story. What are these people like? Match the names with the adjectives.

1. Diana ___a___   ✓ a. friendly
2. Joe _____   b. nervous
3. Megan _____   c. good looking
4. Rick _____   d. strict

Tell Us About Your First Job

Reader Megan Walker writes in with a story about her first job.

I remember my first job. I worked in an outdoor café one summer. It was called Sunny's. I got free drinks and food. My boss Diana was very friendly, and I got along well with her. Her husband Joe worked there, too, but he was really strict. On my first day, I was late because I got lost on the subway. After that, Joe was never too happy with me.

So, every day I served sandwiches and coffee. The café was really busy all the time. I wasn't a very good server, so I was often nervous. Also, I was always exhausted by the end of the day.

One day, I was really tired, so I asked to go home early. Joe looked angry, but he said, "OK. Fine." I left and went to the subway.

Then I met my friend Rick on the street. He was really good looking, and I liked him a lot. He said, "Do you want to go and eat something?" I said, "Yes. OK. Where?" And he said, "I know a café near here. Let's go there. They have good sandwiches."

So we went back to Sunny's and sat down to eat! We waited for about ten minutes before Joe finally came over to the table. He was very busy, so he didn't look at me. He said, "I'm sorry. One of the servers left early. Are you ready to order?" We stayed for an hour. I was lucky because my boss never saw me, but I had to pay for my sandwich and soda!

– *Megan Walker*
New York City

B Read Megan's story again. Then answer the questions.

1. Where did Megan work? *She worked at Sunny's.* _____

2. How did Megan get to work? _____

3. What kind of food did she serve? _____

4. What was the café like? _____

5. Why did she leave early one day? _____

6. Why did she go back to Sunny's? _____

7. How long did they stay at Sunny's? _____

2 He said, . . .

Writing **A** Read the rest of the story. Rewrite their conversation after they leave the café. Use quoted speech. Add capital letters and correct punctuation (" " , . ?).

Rick and I left the café and talked for a few minutes.

rick asked how did you like the café _Rick asked, "How did you like the café?"_

I said it's nice _____

he said the service wasn't very good _____

I said well one of the servers left early _____

rick said people are so lazy these days _____

I said yes I know _____

But I didn't tell Rick I was the server!

B Think about a time you met a friend for the first time. Answer these questions.

1. How old were you? _____
2. What was your friend's name? _____
3. How did you first meet? What happened? _____
4. What did you say when you first met? I said, " _____ ."
5. What did your friend say? She / He said, " _____ ."

C Now write a story about meeting your friend. Use your ideas from part B.

When we met, I was 13 and _____ . _____

_____

_____

_____

Unit 11 Progress chart

What can you do? Mark the boxes. ☑ = I can . . . ? = I need to review how to . . .	To review, go back to these pages in the Student's Book.
Grammar ☐ make simple past statements and questions with *be*.	108 and 109
☐ ask simple past information questions.	110
Vocabulary ☐ name at least 12 words to describe people or experiences.	108 and 109
☐ name at least 4 new expressions with *go*.	111
☐ name at least 5 new expressions with *get*.	111
Conversation strategies ☐ ask and answer questions to show interest.	112
☐ use *Anyway* to change the topic or end a conversation.	113
Writing ☐ use capitals and punctuation in quoted speech.	115

Fabulous food

Lesson A / **Eating habits**

1 Mmmmm!

Vocabulary | Write the names of the foods. Then find the words in the puzzle. Look in these directions (→ ↓).

1. _meat_

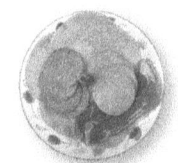
2. _seafood_

3. _____

4. _____

5. _____

7. _____

9. _____

11. _____

13. _____

6. _____

8. _____

10. _____

12. _____

14. _____

F	F	V	C	A	R	R	O	T	S
R	X	E	B	I	B	E	E	F	S
U	O	G	A	X	R	M	E	A	T
I	A	E	N	S	E	I	S	T	A
T	E	T	A	E	A	L	L	C	E
G	G	A	N	A	D	K	F	H	P
P	G	B	A	F	R	U	I	E	P
O	S	L	S	O	P	P	D	E	A
T	F	E	N	O	U	D	L	S	S
A	I	S	Z	D	I	H	G	E	T
T	S	H	R	I	C	E	F	Q	A
O	H	C	H	I	C	K	E	N	M
E	C	U	C	U	M	B	E	R	S
S	H	E	L	L	F	I	S	H	Z

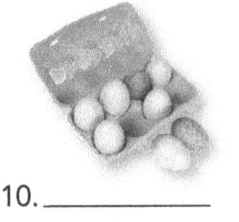

15. _____

16. _____

17. _____

18. _____

2 An invitation to dinner

Grammar **A Read the invitation. Then circle the correct words to complete the emails.**

Invitation to _a housewarming party and dinner_
On _Saturday night at 7:00 p.m._
At _my new apartment!_

Bring a friend. Tell me if you
have food allergies or anything.

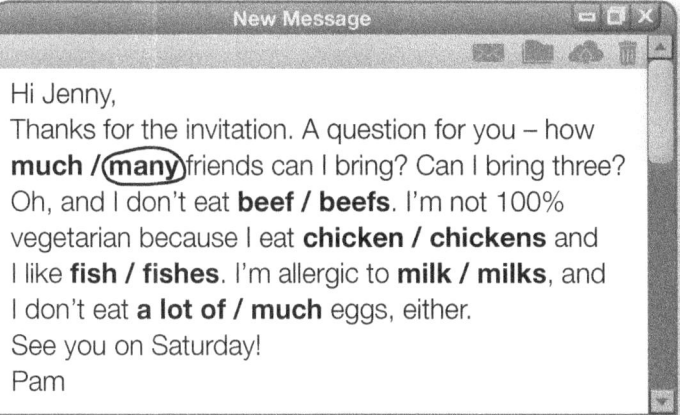

Hi Jenny,
Thanks for the invitation. A question for you – how
much /(many) friends can I bring? Can I bring three?
Oh, and I don't eat **beef / beefs**. I'm not 100%
vegetarian because I eat **chicken / chickens** and
I like **fish / fishes**. I'm allergic to **milk / milks**, and
I don't eat **a lot of / much** eggs, either.
See you on Saturday!
Pam

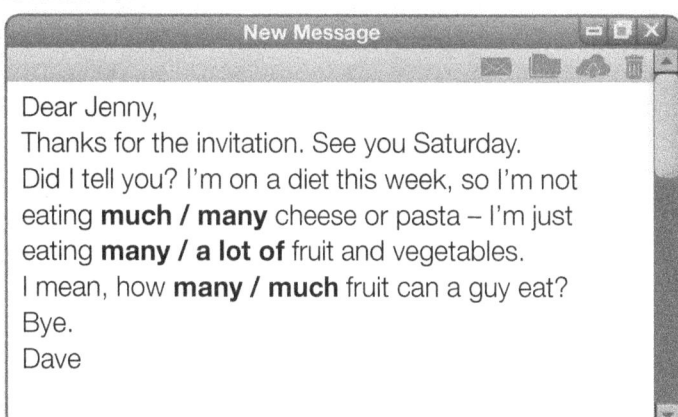

Dear Jenny,
Thanks for the invitation. See you Saturday.
Did I tell you? I'm on a diet this week, so I'm not
eating **much / many** cheese or pasta – I'm just
eating **many / a lot of** fruit and vegetables.
I mean, how **many / much** fruit can a guy eat?
Bye.
Dave

B Write your own email to Jenny. Tell her about these foods.

- food you like
- food you don't like
- food you eat a lot of
- food you don't eat a lot of

New Message

Dear Jenny,
Thanks for the invitation to the party. _____
_____
_____
_____
_____
_____

3 About you

Grammar
and
vocabulary
Complete the questions with *How much* or *How many*. Then write your own answers.

1. _How many_ students in your class are vegetarians? _____
2. _____ milk does your family buy every week? _____
3. _____ times a week do you eat chicken? _____
4. _____ shellfish do you eat? Do you eat a lot? _____
5. _____ of your friends are picky eaters? _____
6. _____ cans of soda do you drink a day? _____

Lesson B — What's for dinner?

1 At the supermarket

Vocabulary | **Write the words under the pictures. Then write the food in the chart below.**

1. _apples_ 2. _____ 3. _____ 4. _____ 5. _____

6. _____ 7. _____ 8. _____ 9. _____ 10. _____

11. _____ 12. _____ 13. _____ 14. _____ 15. _____

16. _____ 17. _____ 18. _____ 19. _____ 20. _____

meat and seafood	fruit	vegetables	other
	apples		

2 What would you like?

Grammar | **Complete the conversations. Use *would you like* or *'d like*.**

1. Jim   What _would you like_ ?

   Megan   I _____ ice cream, please.

   Jim   _____ chocolate sprinkles?

   Megan   Yes, please.

2. Server   Good evening. _____ something to drink?

   Dan   Oh, just water, please.

   Server   OK. And what _____ to eat?

   Dan   Um, I _____ the salmon, please.

   Server   _____ some green beans with it?

   Dan   Actually, I _____ some spinach, please.

3. Greg   Where _____ to go for dinner?

   Sheila   Oh, I don't know. I _____ to go
   somewhere around here.

   Greg   _____ to try the new Thai restaurant?

   Sheila   Oh, yes! I _____ something spicy.

3 *Some* or *any*

Grammar | **Complete the conversations with *some* or *any*.**

1. Ming   Polly, try _some_ lamb.

   Polly   Gosh, it's hot! I need _____ water . . . now!

   Ming   Here. Drink _____ soda.

2. John   Do you have _____ chocolate cookies?

   Ken   No, but we have _____ peanut butter cookies.

   John   OK, I'll take _____ .

3. Sara   Would you like _____ potato chips?

   Craig   Yeah, but I don't have _____ money.

   Sara   Oh, and I don't have _____ , either.

1 Something for lunch

Conversation strategies | **Complete the conversation with *or something* or *or anything*.**

Trish Do you go out for lunch every day or . . . ?

Pete Well, I don't usually eat lunch. I don't like to eat a big meal _or anything_ at lunchtime.

Trish No? You don't have a snack _____ ?

Pete Well, I sometimes have a hot drink, like hot chocolate _____ .

Trish Well, I'm hungry – I'd like a sandwich _____ . Would you like something to eat?

Pete Well, maybe . . .

Trish How about a salad _____ ?

Pete Yes, OK. Actually, I'd like a chicken sandwich. Oh, let's get some ice cream _____ , too. I guess I *am* hungry!

2 About you

Conversation strategies | **Answer the questions. Write true answers. Use *or something* or *or anything*.**

1. Are you a picky eater? | *Well, I don't eat fish or shrimp or anything.*

2. What do you usually have for dinner? | _____

3. How about lunch? | _____

4. What do you like to order in restaurants? | _____

5. What do you drink with meals? | _____

6. What kinds of snacks do you like? | _____

③ Would you like to go out or . . . ?

Conversation
strategies **Complete the conversations. Which questions can end with _or . . . ?_
Add _or . . ._ where possible.**

1. Paul   What would you like for dinner tonight _____ ?
            Would you like to go out _or . . ._ ?

   Val   Yes, please! I'd love to eat out.

   Paul   That's great. So can I choose the restaurant _____ ?

   Val   Sure.

   Paul   Let's see . . . would you like a pizza _____ ?

   Val   Um, I don't want Italian tonight. How about an
            Asian place? Do you like Korean or Thai _____ ?

   Paul   Uh, I don't really care for spicy food.

   Val   Let me think . . . do you want to get a hamburger _____ ?

   Paul   Yeah! With maybe some French fries
            and some cookies.

   Val   OK! Stop! I'm starving! Let's go!

2. Kate   It's my birthday today.

   Sally Happy birthday! Do you have plans _____ ?

   Kate   I had plans, but my friend just called. He's sick.

   Sally That's terrible! I know. Let's eat at my house. I can
            cook some steaks or something. What do you
            think _____ ?

   Kate   That's very nice, thanks, but I'm a vegetarian.

   Sally Oh. Do you eat pasta _____ ?

   Kate   Well, I can't eat pasta or anything heavy right
            now. I'm on a diet.

   Sally OK. No pasta. What would you like _____ ?

   Kate   Do you have any fruit _____ ?

   Sally Sorry. I ate the last banana this morning
            before I went to work. I have some carrots. . . .

   Kate   Let's stop at the supermarket on our way
            to your house.

1 Healthy fast food

Reading | **A Read the blog post. Find the answers to these questions.**

1. Where did the writer eat breakfast? _____
2. What breakfast food does the writer recommend? _____
3. How many calories were in the writer's lunch? _____

TASTES GOOD, AND GOOD FOR YOU!

We often think of fast food as hamburgers, fried chicken, hot dogs, and French fries. However, some fast-food restaurants are starting to offer healthy foods, too. But how healthy is "healthy" fast-food, and how does it taste? I went to some famous fast-food restaurants last week to find the answer and was pleasantly surprised. Here are the two healthy fast-food choices I recommend.

BURGER RESTAURANTS: OATMEAL, PLEASE!

Many burger restaurants open early and serve breakfast, too. One popular restaurant chain has a breakfast with more than 1,000 calories. That's about half the calories you need for a whole day! For a healthy option, you can now choose apple slices (15 calories), fruit and nuts (210 calories), or oatmeal (290 calories). I tried the oatmeal, and it was delicious!

MEXICAN RESTAURANTS: I'D LIKE IT IN A BOWL

I love Mexican fast food as a special treat, but I'm pleased to see that my favorite taco restaurant now has a lot of healthy choices on the menu. A taco salad with beef and cheese is about 600 calories. However, I went for chicken. You can make your own meal with chicken, rice, tomatoes, and other healthy foods. I tried it for lunch. I got it in a bowl and said no to the tortilla chips. It was very tasty and only 450 calories.

Do you know any great, healthy fast-food places? Tell us in the comments section.

B Read the blog post again. Then choose the correct words to complete these sentences.

1. The writer wanted to try some **hamburgers / healthy food** last week.
2. He thinks that 1,000 calories **is / is not** a lot for breakfast.
3. He **enjoyed / didn't enjoy** the oatmeal.
4. He had **taco salad / chicken** for lunch.
5. He **ate / didn't eat** tortilla chips with his lunch.
6. His lunch was **very / not very** healthy.

2 Restaurant reviews

A Jill Heacock is a restaurant reviewer. She ate at the Seafood Palace last week, and she loved it. Circle the correct words to complete Jill's review.

THIS WEEK'S RESTAURANT: **THE SEAFOOD PALACE**   ★ ★ ★ ★

by Jill Heacock

Last week, I went to the Seafood Palace – it's a **terrible /(wonderful)** restaurant. I loved it. I was there on a busy night, and the atmosphere was **fun / formal**. The food was **awful / delicious**, and every dish came to the table **cold / hot**. I really liked the shrimp. Very tasty! The service was **excellent / slow**, the servers were really **friendly / lazy**, and the meal was **cheap / expensive**. I only spent $12!

The Seafood Palace is a good place to hang out with friends or have dinner with your family. Try it!

B Imagine you are a restaurant reviewer. You ate at a restaurant, and you hated it. Write your review.

THIS WEEK'S RESTAURANT: _____   ★

by _____

Last week, I went to _____ – it's a terrible restaurant! _____

_____

_____

_____

_____

_____

Unit 12 Progress chart

What can you do? Mark the boxes. ✓ = I can . . . ? = I need to review how to . . .	To review, go back to these pages in the Student's Book.
Grammar ☐ use countable and uncountable nouns.	118 and 119
☐ make statements and questions with *much, many,* and *a lot of.*	118 and 119
☐ make statements and questions with *some, any,* and *not any.*	120 and 121
☐ make offers and requests with *would like.*	121
Vocabulary ☐ name at least 5 categories of food.	118 and 119
☐ name at least 25 different foods.	118, 119, and 120
Conversation strategies ☐ use *or something* and *or anything.*	122
☐ use *or . . . ?* in *yes-no* questions to make them less direct.	123
Writing ☐ use expressions to talk about restaurants.	124 and 125

Illustration credits

Photo credits

Text credits

The top 500 spoken words

This is a list of the top 500 words in spoken North American English. It is based on a sample of four and a half million words of conversation from the Cambridge International Corpus. The most frequent word, *I*, is at the top of the list.

1. I	40. really	79. see
2. and	41. with	80. how
3. the	42. he	81. they're
4. you	43. one	82. kind
5. uh	44. are	83. here
6. to	45. this	84. from
7. a	46. there	85. did
8. that	47. I'm	86. something
9. it	48. all	87. too
10. of	49. if	88. more
11. yeah	50. no	89. very
12. know	51. get	90. want
13. in	52. about	91. little
14. like	53. at	92. been
15. they	54. out	93. things
16. have	55. had	94. an
17. so	56. then	95. you're
18. was	57. because	96. said
19. but	58. go	97. there's
20. is	59. up	98. I've
21. it's	60. she	99. much
22. we	61. when	100. where
23. huh	62. them	101. two
24. just	63. can	102. thing
25. oh	64. would	103. her
26. do	65. as	104. didn't
27. don't	66. me	105. other
28. that's	67. mean	106. say
29. well	68. some	107. back
30. for	69. good	108. could
31. what	70. got	109. their
32. on	71. OK	110. our
33. think	72. people	111. guess
34. right	73. now	112. yes
35. not	74. going	113. way
36. um	75. were	114. has
37. or	76. lot	115. down
38. my	77. your	116. we're
39. be	78. time	117. any

The top 500 spoken words

118. he's	161. five	204. sort
119. work	162. always	205. great
120. take	163. school	206. bad
121. even	164. look	207. we've
122. those	165. still	208. another
123. over	166. around	209. car
124. probably	167. anything	210. true
125. him	168. kids	211. whole
126. who	169. first	212. whatever
127. put	170. does	213. twenty
128. years	171. need	214. after
129. sure	172. us	215. ever
130. can't	173. should	216. find
131. pretty	174. talking	217. care
132. gonna	175. last	218. better
133. stuff	176. thought	219. hard
134. come	177. doesn't	220. haven't
135. these	178. different	221. trying
136. by	179. money	222. give
137. into	180. long	223. I'd
138. went	181. used	224. problem
139. make	182. getting	225. else
140. than	183. same	226. remember
141. year	184. four	227. might
142. three	185. every	228. again
143. which	186. new	229. pay
144. home	187. everything	230. try
145. will	188. many	231. place
146. nice	189. before	232. part
147. never	190. though	233. let
148. only	191. most	234. keep
149. his	192. tell	235. children
150. doing	193. being	236. anyway
151. cause	194. bit	237. came
152. off	195. house	238. six
153. I'll	196. also	239. family
154. maybe	197. use	240. wasn't
155. real	198. through	241. talk
156. why	199. feel	242. made
157. big	200. course	243. hundred
158. actually	201. what's	244. night
159. she's	202. old	245. call
160. day	203. done	246. saying

The top 500 spoken words

247. dollars	290. started	333. believe
248. live	291. job	334. thinking
249. away	292. says	335. funny
250. either	293. play	336. state
251. read	294. usually	337. until
252. having	295. wow	338. husband
253. far	296. exactly	339. idea
254. watch	297. took	340. name
255. week	298. few	341. seven
256. mhm	299. child	342. together
257. quite	300. thirty	343. each
258. enough	301. buy	344. hear
259. next	302. person	345. help
260. couple	303. working	346. nothing
261. own	304. half	347. parents
262. wouldn't	305. looking	348. room
263. ten	306. someone	349. today
264. interesting	307. coming	350. makes
265. am	308. eight	351. stay
266. sometimes	309. love	352. mom
267. bye	310. everybody	353. sounds
268. seems	311. able	354. change
269. heard	312. we'll	355. understand
270. goes	313. life	356. such
271. called	314. may	357. gone
272. point	315. both	358. system
273. ago	316. type	359. comes
274. while	317. end	360. thank
275. fact	318. least	361. show
276. once	319. told	362. thousand
277. seen	320. saw	363. left
278. wanted	321. college	364. friends
279. isn't	322. ones	365. class
280. start	323. almost	366. already
281. high	324. since	367. eat
282. somebody	325. days	368. small
283. let's	326. couldn't	369. boy
284. times	327. gets	370. paper
285. guy	328. guys	371. world
286. area	329. god	372. best
287. fun	330. country	373. water
288. they've	331. wait	374. myself
289. you've	332. yet	375. run

The top 500 spoken words

376. they'll	418. company	460. sorry
377. won't	419. friend	461. living
378. movie	420. set	462. drive
379. cool	421. minutes	463. outside
380. news	422. morning	464. bring
381. number	423. between	465. easy
382. man	424. music	466. stop
383. basically	425. close	467. percent
384. nine	426. leave	468. hand
385. enjoy	427. wife	469. gosh
386. bought	428. knew	470. top
387. whether	429. pick	471. cut
388. especially	430. important	472. computer
389. taking	431. ask	473. tried
390. sit	432. hour	474. gotten
391. book	433. deal	475. mind
392. fifty	434. mine	476. business
393. months	435. reason	477. anybody
394. women	436. credit	478. takes
395. month	437. dog	479. aren't
396. found	438. group	480. question
397. side	439. turn	481. rather
398. food	440. making	482. twelve
399. looks	441. American	483. phone
400. summer	442. weeks	484. program
401. hmm	443. certain	485. without
402. fine	444. less	486. moved
403. hey	445. must	487. gave
404. student	446. dad	488. yep
405. agree	447. during	489. case
406. mother	448. lived	490. looked
407. problems	449. forty	491. certainly
408. city	450. air	492. talked
409. second	451. government	493. beautiful
410. definitely	452. eighty	494. card
411. spend	453. wonderful	495. walk
412. happened	454. seem	496. married
413. hours	455. wrong	497. anymore
414. war	456. young	498. you'll
415. matter	457. places	499. middle
416. supposed	458. girl	500. tax
417. worked	459. happen	